TITANIC
UNINTENDED CONSEQUENCES

by
DICK SHEPPARD

The law of unintended consequences states that any action taken to modify a complex system will create unanticipated outcomes that, often times, will be undesirable.

TITANIC
UNINTENDED CONSEQUENCES

by
DICK SHEPPARD

Copyright © 2011 Richard Sheppard
All rights Reserved

ISBN: 0-615-51004-3
ISBN-13:978-0-615-51004-0
LCCN:2011911827

To my dad who loved the sea, rest in peace.

I miss you dad.

CONTENTS

PREFACE i

TITANIC URBAN LEGEND 1

THE ICEBERG THAT HIT THE TITANIC 7

CONTINUOUS GASH THEORY 21

STEAM BOILERS & ELECTRICITY 33

LISTING TO PORT 37

POINT OF CONTACT 53

LEGEND VS THEORY 67

EXPLOSIONS 83

300 FOOT GASH VS. GROUNDING THEORY 93

WHAT REALLY HAPPENED THAT NIGHT 101

UNINTENDED CONSEQUENCES 115

ACKNOWLEDGEMENTS 127

BIBLIOGRAPHY 129

END NOTES 131

PREFACE

I was born on September 29, 1946; thirty-four years, five months and fourteen days after the Titanic sank, taking with her 1,503 souls to the great hereafter. For whatever reason, the story of the sinking of this ship has fascinated me since 1953, when my father took me to see the film *Titanic*, staring Clifton Webb and Barbara Stanwyck. From that day on, I found myself obsessed with the subject as I built several models of the *Titanic*, collected memorabilia and read every book about the *Titanic* that I could get my hands on.

After seeing the 1953 film, I remember lying awake at night trying to imagine what it must have been like going down with the ship. I wondered about what went through everyone's mind as they realized that they were bound for eternity. Why did the *Titanic* sink so rapidly leading to the death of so many people before a rescue ship could arrive? Why did the passengers on the *Titanic* think the ship was unsinkable? Why were there not enough lifeboats? As an ever curious seven-year old, I even found myself speculating as to how long a person could hold his breath under water, which was only one of the questions with which I would lull myself to sleep.

Much to my delight, a new film called *A Night To Remember* hit the silver screen in 1958. There I was again seated in the first row of the movie theater with my box of popcorn, convinced that this account would be more factual than the love story I had seen with my father five years before. However, after the film, the same questions remained, particularly one: Why had she sunk so fast? I understood that when the ship had lost five of her watertight compartments, she was doomed. But could an iceberg really have cut open the side of the ship in such a way as to flood those supposedly impregnable units?

Finally, Dr. Robert Ballard, Senior Scientist, Woods Hole Oceanographic Institute, began to shed light on the mystery when he discovered the final resting place of the *Titanic* in 1985. Like everyone else, I marveled at the pictures that were published and quickly purchased my tiny piece of coal from the Titanic Society that had been brought up from the wreck. As the investigations continued, there surfaced a plausible explanation as to what sank the *Titanic*. In 1996, an ultra sound investigation using a sub-bottom profiler was conducted on the starboard bow and hull of the *Titanic* below the mud. Six non-continuous cracks, totaling to 235 feet, were discovered on the starboard hull of the ship. At last, this new discovery seemed to explain how the sea had entered so many compartments simultaneously.

In 1997, the next *Titanic* film, hit the silver screen. This film seemed to follow the most recent data discovered from analyzing the Titanic wreck, in particular the fact that she had broken in half. The new film was absolutely breathtaking and wowed the audience with computer-enhanced images of the *Titanic* crossing the Atlantic and ultimately sinking by the bow. But the question still remained, was the film correct?

That question was answered in 2005 with the discovery by of what were believed to be the sections of the bottom and tank top of the *Titanic* resting on the ocean floor by John Chatterton and Richie Kohler. It would now appear that the reason the *Titanic* sank so quickly was because she had somehow lost a large section of her bottom and broken apart on the surface.

Shortly after the discovery of the bottom pieces of the *Titanic*, I was fortunate enough to win a bid on EBay® for the 1912 first edition book, *Sinking Of The Titanic, Thrilling Stories Told By Survivors*, by Jay Henry Mowbray, PHD, LL.D. After reading that account, I quickly realized that everything I had thought about the sinking of the *Titanic* was based on the films I had seen and were more often than not, incorrect assumptions.

It seemed to me that the *Titanic* had become an "urban legion" that had been fabricated over the years by Hollywood films, which simply ignored many of the real events that occurred on April 14-15, 1912. Unfortunately, the Hollywood film industry was not alone in ignoring the facts. Even in 1912, the United States Titanic Disaster Hearings in New York disregarded eyewitness accounts of the ship breaking in half on the surface and concluded that the ship had gone down in one piece, which no doubt accounted for the accounting of the disaster as it appeared in the 1953 and 1958 films.

Boiler explosions were also discounted by the committee simply because Second Officer Charles Herbert Lightoller and others said the steam had been vented in the boilers, and yet, the Titanic's lights remained on throughout the sinking and right up to her final plunge. Somehow the investigating committees and Hollywood forgot to ask how the ship's electricity was generated. Incredible though it seems, both the investigating committee of 1912 and subsequently Hollywood had not considered the fact that steam boilers powered the dynamos with steam at 182 psi and kept the lights burning until they exploded right before she broke in half and took her final plunge into history.

Unlike other books that have been written, there will be no attempt in these pages to place blame on anyone for their actions or lack thereof on that faithful night. It is not my purpose to determine if Captain Smith recklessly plowed head on into an ice flow, or if Ismay, the managing director of the White Star Line, instructed Captain Smith after the collision to restart the engines to get to Halifax, nor is it my intention to place the blame for the massive loss of life on Captain Stanley Lord of the *Californian*, whose ship was stopped dead in the ice flow approximately ten miles away from the *Titanic* and remained in his warm bunk as hundreds of people drowned or froze to death?

It is important to remember that all of the main characters of this event either went down with the *Titanic* or died of old age. These people can no longer address the charges that have been made against them. Consequently, it is unacceptable to theorize as to the exact cause of the sinking of the ship, which took them to their death based on unsubstantiated evidence.

Ninety-nine years after the sinking, all we can know for certain are the words of the 705 survivors that are forever immortalized on cold pieces of ageing paper or immortalized on audio recordings. As a consequence, I will depend exclusively on eyewitness accounts of the survivors and recent physical evidence discovered at the wreck, in an attempt to set the record straight as to what actually happened on that faithful night and allow the reader to draw their conclusions as to why the *Titanic* sank free of any opinions of the author.

Actually, we will never really know what went on that fateful night for the simple reason that most of the very people who actually "saw" what happened, the firemen, stokers, greasers, trimmers and engineers, who toiled in the belly of the Titanic, Captain Smith and Thomas Andrews, the ships Captain and designer, never made it off the ship alive.

But in all actuality, the story of what happened to what was then the largest passenger ship in the world has been with us for over ninety-nine years hidden away in the depths of the Atlantic Ocean, in the memories of those who survived its sinking, the few who have left their accounts in print or in audio transcripts that echo back to that fateful night, demanding the attention they so rightfully deserve. Thanks to the discovery of the debris field between the bow and stern sections of the *Titanic*, we have conclusive proof that the ship did not go down in one piece, but rather broke in half as a result of boiler explosions which ripped her tank top asunder, resulting in her breaking in half on the surface of the ocean and subsequently to sink before any rescue ships could save her doomed passengers.

The pages that you are about to read, tells a story that may put an end to the "urban legend" created by Hollywood and may explain what really did happen that night by pointing out the "unintended consequences" of decisions that were made prior to the ship's launching and actions that were taken by the crew on the night of April 14, 1912 and early morning of April 15, 1912. These "unintended consequences" overwhelmed the *Titanic* like a perfect storm and prematurely sent her to a watery grave. May the mighty *Titanic* and the 1,503 souls that went down with her forever rest in eternal peace.

CHAPTER ONE
THE TITANIC URBAN LEGEND

The *Titanic* was a glorious ship that was built by Harland & Wolff in Belfast, Northern Ireland. Work commenced in July 1907. At the time, there would be two ships, the *Olympic* and the *Titanic* built side by side and eventually, there would be a third, the *Britannic*. Work on *Titanic's* keel began on March 31, 1909 and on May 31, 1911, her hull was launched and towed to the Thompson Graving Dock to be fitted out with her propellers, final hull painting and completion of the interior. When she was completed, the *Titanic* was eight hundred and eighty-two feet, nine inches long, with a beam of ninety-two feet, six inches and a draft of thirty-four feet. She was one hundred and seventy-five feet from the keel to the top of her four stacks and weighed in at forty-six thousand, three hundred and twenty eight gross registered tons. Her hull was constructed with one inch steel plates that were held in place by three million rivets. Her official yard number given to her by Harland and Wolff was 401, a number that Dr. Robert Ballard would photograph on the ships propeller in 1985, conclusively proving that he had found the famous wreck.

The *RMS Titanic*, a double-bottomed ship, had two, two hundred and ninety-six foot long bilge keel placed amidships, port and starboard, to prevent rolling at sea. The ship was electrified by steam-powered dynamos that provided electricity to over ten thousand electric light bulbs, elevators, cranes and heaters throughout the ship. The *Titanic* also had a powerful 5 kW, three hundred and fifty mile range; Marconi Wireless Radio manned twenty-four hours a day by two men.

The ship was steam powered having twenty nine coal stoked boilers that powered two reciprocating four cylinder direct drive inverted steam engines for the two outside propellers and one low pressure Parsons Turbine for the center propeller that would provide her with a top speed capability of 25 knots at seventy-eight revolutions per minute, a speed she would never reach. For her maiden voyage to New York, she was loaded with 5,892 tons of coal.

Safety was addressed not only by fifteen transverse watertight bulkheads forming sixteen watertight compartments, secured with watertight doors that could be closed from the bridge electrically, manually with a hand crank, gravity by pulling a release pin and automatically by a water sensor float that would close the door if there were water present and a double bottom, but also by twenty lifeboats, four more than required by the Board of Trade, consisting of two emergency lifeboats (forty people each), fourteen lifeboats (sixty-five people each) and four Engelhardt Collapsible boats (forty-nine people each). The total number of seats available on the lifeboats was a one thousand, one hundred and seventy-eight.

For the enjoyment of her passengers, the *Titanic* boasted twenty-eight First Class suites, a swimming pool, four electric elevators, an indoor squash court, two libraries, four restaurants, three galleys, two musical ensembles, a fully equipped gym, one barber shop, a fully equipped dark-room, two physicians and one operating room.

On her maiden voyage, the *Titanic* carried three hundred and twenty-nine First Class, two hundred and eighty-five Second Class and seven hundred and ten Third Class passengers. She was manned by eight hundred and ninety-nine crewmembers, bringing the number of souls aboard to two thousand, two hundred and twenty-three.

Shortly after high noon on a chilly 47-degree day, April 10, 1912, the *Titanic* sounded her deep throated whistle and began her maiden voyage, narrowly missing, in the process, a collision with the docked passenger ship, the *New* York which, because of the suction created by the immense size of the vessel as she passed through the narrow harbor, succeeded in ripping the smaller ship from its moorings. Surviving the narrow miss, the *Titanic* arrived in Cherbourg, France to pick up additional passengers at 8:10 PM, she lifted anchor and sailed for Queenstown, Ireland. 11:30 AM the following day, the *Titanic* dropped anchor in Queenstown Harbor, picked up more passengers and more mail. At 1:30 PM, she lifted her starboard anchor for the last time to begin her voyage to New York, passing Old Head of Kinsale as she headed out to sea and into the pages of glory.[1]

At first, the cruse to New York seemed remarkably uneventful. The sea was calm and the passengers were enjoying the splendor of the ship. Thomas Andrews, managing director and head of the drafting department for the shipbuilding company Harland and Wolff conducted watertight door closing drills as the wireless operators repaired the Marconi Wireless radio that had broken down. The *Titanic* steamed 386 miles on the first full day at sea.[2]

On April 13th, Captain Smith began his daily inspection of the ship. The coal bunker fire in boiler room six that had plagued them from the beginning of the voyage had finally been put out. There were signs of heat damage to the steel bulkhead and Captain Smith ordered that it be rubbed down with oil. In the last twenty-four hours, the *Titanic* had traveled 519 miles.[3]

From April 13th noon until 11:40 AM on April 14th the Titanic travel another 546 miles, leaving approximately another 250 miles to go before meeting her fate.[4] Prior to that however, the *Titanic* received an ice warning from the *Carolina* and Dutch liner *Noordam*. By early afternoon, she received another ice warning from the *Baltic* saying that there were large quantities of field ice directly in the path of the *Titanic*. Later on that afternoon, another ice warning is received from the *Amerika*. For whatever reason, Captain Smith never received this warning; however he did alter the ships course, taking her further south, but for whatever reason, did not reduce speed. At approximately 7:30 PM, the *Californian* sent a third message to the Titanic saying that there was ice approximately fifty miles ahead.[5]

At approximately 9:20 PM, Captain Smith left the bridge to retire for the night leaving Second Officer Lightoller to continue his watch. The lookouts were instructed to be on the lookout for ice. The *Titanic* was now cruising at approximately 21 to 22 knots, although the precise speed is not known for certain since the ships log went down with the ship. Around 9:30 PM, a message was received from the ship *Masaba* warning of a heavy ice pack and icebergs ahead, a message which was ignored by the wireless operators as they continued to send out the usual communications from the *Titanic* passengers. At 10:00 PM, Second Officer Lightoller was relieved by First Officer Murdoch. The *Titanic* was running at a speed of approximately 22 knots with 24 of her 29 boilers in full operation. At 10:55 PM and ten to twenty miles ahead of the *Titanic,* the *Californian* tried to send a message to the *Titanic* saying that she had stopped dead in the water because of ice.[6] Wireless operator Phillips interrupted the incoming message and replied to the *Californian* with a blistering assault telling her to, *"Keep out! Shut up! You're jamming my signal! I am working Cape Race!"*[7] The wireless operator of the *Californian* turned off his radio and went to bed.

The air temperature continued to fall and a concerned Murdoch issued orders for the fresh water tanks to be checked for freezing. Approximately 11:40 PM, Frederick Fleet, the lookout, rang the bell in the crow's nest three times and screamed into the telephone to Sixth Officer Moody, "Iceberg right ahead!" The message was relayed to Murdoch who yelled, "Hard a-starboard". Reaching for the ships Engine Order Telegraph, E.O.T., he signaled the engine room, "Full Stop" and then issues a second command "Full Astern".[8]

The *Titanic* gradually began to turn to port but regrettably hit the iceberg with a glancing blow 37 seconds later and ripped a continuous gash into her starboard side approximately three hundred feet long, beginning at the bow and continuing to boiler room five. Murdoch immediately issued orders to close the watertight doors and yelled to helmsman Robert Hitchens "full to port" in an attempt to corner the ship around the remainder of the iceberg. As ice fell onto the Forecastle deck of the *Titanic*, Captain Smith entered the bridge and Murdoch informed him that they had struck an iceberg. It is approximately 11:40 PM.[9]

By 12:00 AM, the post office on G deck is flooded. Thomas Andrews informed the Captain that the first five water tight compartments were flooded to the waterline and the ship would surely flounder. Officer Boxhall, at the instruction of Captain Smith, calculated the ship's position, 41.46° N, 51.14° W and Captain Smith rushed to the wireless room and ordered Phillips to send out a CQD distress call. By 12:05 AM on the morning of April 15, 1912, the squash court was flooded and the water was within 19.6 feet of the top deck of the *Titanic*. At 12:15 AM, the steamer *Carpathia* answered the *Titanic* distress call. She was approximately 58 miles away and would arrive in four hours. Unfortunately, the *Titanic* would flounder in two hours and thirteen minutes.[10]

At 12:25 PM, Captain Smith ordered the lifeboats to be filled with women and children, thus beginning the final act of what seemed to be a modern day Greek tragedy. With Second Officer Lightoller on the port side and First Officer Murdoch on the starboard side, the process of loading the lifeboats with passengers began. Between the hours of 12:25 AM and 2:20

AM, a ship was seen on the distant horizon. Officer Boxhall was instructed by Captain Smith to fire distress rockets into the starry sky and to use the Morris Lamp to communicate with the distant ship that appeared to be only about ten to twenty miles away. To their dismay, the distant ship did not respond as the last of the lifeboats were lowered, partially filled, into the inky black sea. At 2:18 AM, the lights flickered out for the last time aboard the *Titanic* and she ripped apart at the third funnel. Moments later at 2:21 AM, the stern section disappeared beneath the waves.[11] For those that did not drown, the 28° F made their passage into eternity a numbing experience as they quickly froze to death.

At 3:30 AM, the *Carpathia's* rockets were observed by the survivors in the lifeboats. Lifeboat 2 was received first by the *Carpathia* at 4:10 AM and by 8:30 AM; the final lifeboat was rescued with Second Officer Lightoller being the last of the 705 survivors to be brought aboard the ship. All told, 1,595 people died on the morning of April 15, 1912 and on April 18, 1912, the Carpathia arrived in New York at 9:00 PM and discharged the survivors.[12]

Whereas the Titanic was not the largest sea disaster in terms of loss of life, it has gone down in history as being one of the worst and certainly the most publicized sea disaster in maritime history.

CHAPTER TWO
THE ICEBERG THAT HIT THE TITANIC

Of the many facets of the *Titanic* "urban legend" that should be addressed, one of the most important is the size of the iceberg that sank the ship. Since 1953, Hollywood has constantly portrayed the iceberg as being a towering structure that hid in the darkness until the *Titanic* approached closely enough for it to strike its lethal blow.

In the 20th Century Fox production of the film *Titanic*, we see a mammoth iceberg being calved from a glacier somewhere along the Greenland coast and carried south in the cold Labrador Current on its way to met the *Titanic*. In this film, The *Titanic*, like a bowling ball hitting a single ten pin, crossed the Atlantic and ran headlong into this single iceberg. The movie gives the impression that the tragedy occurred because of the "hubris implicit" in calling the *Titanic "unsinkable"*. In this 1953 film, the berg towered above the main mast of the ship, which was a full seventy-five feet taller than the four funnels. Since the top of the funnels measured from the keel was one hundred and seventy five feet and the draft of the ship was thirty-four feet, six inches, the iceberg itself would have had to measure over two hundred and fifteen feet, six inches tall from the waterline of the Titanic. Since eight-ninths of the berg was submersed beneath the waves, the burg itself would have had to measure over one thousand, nine hundred and thirty-nine and one half feet tall! On top of this, the film makes the major mistake of showing the Titanic hitting the iceberg on its "port" side, not its "starboard" side.

In the 1958, The Rank Organization, William Mac Quitty Production of the film *A Night To Remember*, the iceberg is shown towering above the Forecastle and Shelter C decks as the *Titanic* collides with the iceberg on her starboard side. In the 1958 film, you really cannot see the top of the berg as you could in the 1953 film *Titanic*, but from its dimensions as it passes by, it is easy to see that it is much higher than the Bridge, and considerably higher than the boat deck. At the time of the collision, the Titanic displaced 52,310 tons and the Boat Deck was 58 feet above the waterline.[13] This would mean that the berg was much higher than 58 feet, a point that is not supported by testimony given by the eyewitnesses.

Finally, in the 1997 film, *Titanic*, we are again presented with an enormous iceberg that seemingly towers above the *Titanic*. In this film, we know it is as tall as the Boat Deck as we see Officer Murdoch looking directly at the side of the berg from the wheelhouse as the ship hits the iceberg. From Murdoch's vantage point, he is 58 feet above the waterline, the iceberg seems to be considerably higher. So we see that, once again, the height of the berg shown in the film is far greater than that described by witnesses. As in the case before, the iceberg shown in the film is not in agreement with the eyewitnesses.

The problem with all of this, of course, is the fact that the portion of the iceberg that was above the water line was considerably smaller than what Hollywood would like us to believe. Perhaps in Hollywood where, "bigger is better" filmmakers are compelled to use their special effects departments to impress their audiences. But given eyewitness accounts of the physical dimensions of the iceberg, the film representation is simply not true.

During his testimony before the Titanic Disaster Hearings in Washington, D.C., Tuesday, April 23, 1912, Witness Frederick Fleet, Able seaman and *Titanic* Lookout, gave the following testimony in response to questions asked by Senator Smith.

"Senator Smith: I wish you would tell the committee whether you apprehended danger when you sounded these signals and telephoned; whether you thought there was danger?

Mr. Fleet: No: no, sir. That is all we have to do up in the nest to ring the bell, and if there is any danger ring them up on the telephone.

Senator Smith: The fact that you did ring them up on the telephone indicated that you thought there was danger?

Mr. Fleet: Yes, sir.

Senator Smith: You thought there was danger?

Mr. Fleet: Well it was close to us. That is why I rang them up.

Senator Smith: How large an object was it?

Mr. Fleet: It was not very large when I first saw it.

Senator Smith: How large was it?

Mr. Fleet: I have no idea of distances or spaces.

Senator Smith: Was it as large as the table at which I am sitting?

Mr. Fleet: It would be as large as those two tables put together, when I saw it first.

Senator Smith: When you first saw it, it appeared about as large as these two tables put together?

Mr. Fleet: Yes, sir.

Senator Smith: Did it appear to get larger after you saw it?

Mr. Fleet: Yes, it kept getting larger as we were getting nearer it.

Senator Smith: As it was coming toward you and you were going toward it?

Mr. Fleet: Yes.

Senator Smith: How large did it get to be, finally when it struck the ship?

Mr. Fleet: When we were alongside, it was a little bit higher than the forecastle head.

Senator Smith: The forecastle head is how high above the water line?

Mr. Fleet: Fifty feet, I should say.

Senator Smith: About 50 feet?

Mr. Fleet: Yes.

Senator Smith: So this black mass, when it finally struck the boat, turned out to be about 50 feet above the water?

Mr. Fleet: About 50 or 60.

Senator Smith: Fifty of sixty feet above the water?

Mr. Fleet: Yes.

Senator Smith: And when you first saw it looked no larger than these two tables.

Mr. Fleet: No, sir."[14]

During the British Wreck Commissioner's Inquiry, Fleet testified:

"17301, what did you see when that happened? Your vessel, as I understand you, was going port. Then you say she struck an iceberg. Tell us what you saw. You were in the crow's-nest, watching it were you not?

- Yes

17302. Did you see any ice come on deck?

- Yes, some on the forecastle head and some on the well deck.

17303. Could you tell how high, at all, the berg was?

- No, I could not.

17304. You could not tell us in feet, of course, or measurement in that was, but can you give us any idea; was it as high as you were?

Just a little bit higher than the forecastle head.

17305 (The Commissioner), Now someone can tell me how high from the water was the forecastle head?

I do not know.

The Commissioner: No, you cannot; but someone can.

The Attorney General: About 40 to 50 feet, I think.

Sir Robert Finlay: About 55 feet, My Lord.

17306. (The Commissioner – To the Witness) This berg that you struck must have been higher than the forecastle head because ice fell from it on to the forecastle head and on to the well deck, so I suppose it must have been higher than the forecastle head. That would be so, would it not?

- Yes.

173067. Now how much above the forecastle head did this berg stand, about. Can you show me in this room, I mean. If you cannot, do not try?

- No, I do not know.

The Commissioner: It is far better to say you do not know.

17308. (The attorney General – To the witness.) You will tell me if you can?

- I cannot say; I do not know.

17309. Was it as high as you were on the crow's-nest"

No, it was not.

17310. Not as high as that?

No.

17311. But above the forecastle head?

Yes.

Sir Robert Finlay: Mr. Wilding has just verified it again, and finds it was 55 feet above the waterline.

The Attorney General: I think the crow's-nest is about 40 feet above the deck.

Sir Robert Finlay: Above the forecastle, yes.

The Attorney General: One can form some impression of height.

The Commissioner: In the crow's nest you know he would be looking down upon this when it struck, and not looking up to it. He said the berg was not as high as the crow's nest.

The Attorney General: Yes, he is quite clear about that. What I have got from him is: It was not as high as the crow's nest, but it was higher than the forecastle head, and that is about as much as we could expect to get.

The Commissioner: It may have been standing about 75 feet above the surface of the water."[15]

What Fleet was describing to Senator Smith and to the British inquiry was a small to medium size iceberg. A small iceberg is defined as having a height of fourteen to fifty feet in height and a length of forty-seven to two hundred feet long while the larger medium size iceberg would be forty-nine to one hundred and forty eight feet high and two hundred to three hundred and ninety feet long. The iceberg that hit the *Titanic* did not, as dramatized in Hollywood films, tower above the mast or Bridge of the *Titanic*, it cleared the rail on Shelter Deck C, thirty feet, six inches above the water line and remained below the crow's nest that was ninety-five feet from the surface of the water. The Commissioner during the British Titanic Wreck hearings was more than likely incorrect in saying that the iceberg was probably 75 feet high since the Boat Deck, according to the British Wreck Commission report, was only fifty-eight feet above the waterline. This measurement would therefore make the iceberg as tall as the Boat Deck and the bridge and is fairly consistent with the testimony of Edith Russell who was a first class passenger on A deck, room A11. She stated that when she was entering her stateroom from an inside corridor, she felt series of three bumps. She went directly to the promenade deck using another door in her stateroom and observed what she described as "a large gray building" that was floating by.[16] The promenade deck was one deck below the boat deck, which was fifty-eight feet above the waterline.

Quartermaster Alfred Olliver who was on the compass platform located between the second and third funnels on the Boat Deck, nine feet above Edith Russell's deck, heard the three warning bells made by Fleet. Olliver left the compass platform and started toward the bow on the port side and saw the peak of the iceberg passing the bridge heading astern.

Fourth Officer Joseph Groves Boxhall, testified on the Day Three of the Inquiries by the US Senate that,

"*Mr. Boxhall: We all walked out to the corner of the bridge then top look at the iceberg.*

Senator Smith: The Captain?

Mr. Boxhall: The Captain, first officer and myself.

Senator Smith: Did you see it?

Mr. Boxhall: I was not very sure of seeing it. It seemed to me to be just a small black mass not rising very high out of the water, just a little on the starboard quarter.

Senator Smith: How far out of the water should you judge?

Mr. Boxhall: I could not judge the size of it, but it seemed to me to be very, very low-lying.

Senator Smith: Did it extend up to B Deck?

Mr. Boxhall: Oh, no; the ship was past it then. It looked to me to be very, very low in the water.

Senator Fletcher: Give us an idea; do not leave it there.

Senator Smith: How far do you think it was above the water?

Mr. Boxhall: That is hard to say. In my opinion I do not think the thing extended above the ship's rail.

Senator Smith: Above the ship's rail?

Mr. Boxhall: No.

Senator Smith: And how far was this rail above the water's edge?

Mr. Boxhall: Probably about thirty feet.

Senator Smith: About thirty feet.

Mr. Boxhall: No; hardly thirty feet.

Senator Smith: The distance from the water's edge to the boat deck was how far?

Mr. Boxhall: I could get that measurement from the plan.

Senator Smith: About seventy feet, was it not?

Mr. Boxhall: From the boat deck it was about seventy feet to the water's edge. The boat deck is one deck above A. The rail I mean is on the C deck."

George A. Harder, 25, Brooklyn manufacturer and first-class passenger testified on Day Twelve of the hearings in New York that, "… at 20 minutes to 12 we were not asleep yet, and I heard a dull thump. Then I could feel the boat quiver and could feel a sort of rumbling, scraping noise along the side of the boat. When I went to the porthole I saw this iceberg go by. The porthole was closed. The iceberg was, I should say, about 50 to 100 feet away. I should say it was about as high as the top deck of the boat. I just got a glimpse of it, and it is hard to tell how high it was."[17]

It is clear to see that the *Titanic* hit an iceberg that was rather small in size, was a blue berg, and disappeared into the night, never to be seen again.

BLUE ICEBERGS

What is a "blue" berg? Icebergs are calved from glaciers that are thousand's of years old and during the process of their creation, melt water freezes rapidly into ice that has no air bubbles. It is this lack of air bubbles that makes the ice absorb all colors except blue, which it reflects. It is the reflected blue that we see, hence the name "blue iceberg".

The traditional white icebergs that are shown in films about the *Titanic* are formed by years of snowfall on the glacier from which they are calved. Over the years, the snow piles up and, along with the air bubbles, is compacted. It is the trapped air bubbles that reflect all light, thus making the iceberg appear to be white in color. It would be conceivable therefore that a glacier could have a large portion of melt ice on the bottom that was covered by years of snowfall. This would create an iceberg that could have a white and a blue side, depending on which side of the iceberg that was facing the observer.

Icebergs melt at different rates as they head south, driven by the Labrador Current. Since they are formed from glaciers, boulders and other terrestrial debris could be trapped inside of the ice. The mass of the terrestrial material is not affected by the melting of the ice; however, it can have a distinct impact on the stability of the berg in which it is imprisoned.

When the buoyancy of an iceberg shifts, rolling it over, the ice which has been below the water line could be, depending on the composition of the berg itself, blue. This could explain the "black" mass reported by Fleet who first saw the berg from the crow's nest on a dark moonless night. Under these conditions, a "blue" berg would certainly appear to be a "black" mass. Lightoller also testified at the British inquiry that the iceberg had recently "turned turtle" (flipped over). Mr. Edwin Cannons, Master of the Atlantic Transport lines testified that he had once seen an iceberg flip in the daylight. He described the berg as being blue when the white mass turned over revealing the once submerged bottom of the iceberg.[18]

Reginald Lee, *Titanic* lookout who was on duty with Fleet in the crow's nest, gave the most descriptive testimony about the iceberg at the British inquiry saying,

"2442. It was a dark mass that appeared, you say?

Through this haze, and as she moved away from it, there was just a white fringe along the top. That was the only white about it, until she passed by, and then you could see she was white; one side of it seemed to be black, and the other side seemed to be white. When I had a look at it going astern it appeared to be white."[19]

When icebergs "turn turtle", they do not necessarily have to turn 180° with the bottom on the surface and the top, submerged beneath the waves. Since the force that makes the icebergs roll is gravity, and since, as the iceberg melts, the center of gravity shifts with the degree of shift determining the degree of roll. Therefore, it would be conceivable that Lee's description of one side of the iceberg being blue and the other side being white would indicate that the iceberg rolled only 90°, thereby creating a two faced iceberg with the blue section facing Lee and the *Titanic* on that fateful night.

There were reports that an iceberg that was photographed by passengers on the German ship *Prinz Adalbert* the following morning and it was reported to have a dark stripe along the side, the red stripe was of course was supposed to be the red paint of the *Titanic* hull that was painted red below the waterline. This berg however, was much too large and the stripe was on the white section of the iceberg and thus would not match the description provided by Lee, Fleet, Boxhall or Lightoller.

Unfortunately from a historical perspective, there was in 1912, and still is today, a fixation by the majority of the public on the idea that an extraordinarily large iceberg sank the *Titanic*. Reviewing the statements made by some of the 705 *Titanic* survivors who were adrift in their lifeboats, we find that it is their universal agreement that at daybreak, they found themselves looking across the freezing sea and reported seeing countless icebergs of all sizes and a massive ice flow all about.

Mrs. Emily B. Ryerson, a First-Class passenger from Philadelphia, PA stated in her Affidavit read into the record by Senator Smith, *"Then, when the sun rose we saw the Carpathia standing up about 5 miles away, and for the first time saw the icebergs all around us."*[20]

Mr. Moore Captain of the passenger ship *Mount Temple*, Day Eight, Saturday, April 27, Washington D.C. *"I saw a large ice pack right to the east of me, sir; right in my track, right in my course."*

Senator Smith: How large?

Mr. Moore: In consulting my officers as to the breadth of this, one said it was 5 miles and another said it was 6 miles.

Senator Smith: How wide was it?

Mr. Moore: That was the width of it.

Senator Smith: How long was it?

Mr. Moore: I should say 20 miles, perhaps more than that. It was field ice and bergs.

Senator Smith: Bergs also?

Mr. Moore: Yes; bergs interspersed in the pack, sir, and bowlders (boulders, Author's note).

Senator Smith: How many bergs were there?

Mr. Moore: I should say, altogether, there must have been between 40 and 50 I counted that morning…

Senator Smith: How high was the highest, the largest one?

Mr. Moore: I should say fully 200 feet high, sir."[21]

Mr. Author Henry Rostron, Captain of the Canard liner *Carpathia*, First day of the Titanic Disaster Hearings, Friday, April 19, 1912, The Waldorf-Astoria Hotel, New York,

"By the time we had the first boat's people it was breaking day, and then I could see the remaining boats all around within an area of about 4 miles. I also saw icebergs all around me. There were about 20 icebergs that would be anywhere from about 150 to 200 feet high and numerous smaller bergs; also numerous what we call "growlers." You would not call them bergs. They were anywhere from 10 to 12 feet high and 10 to 15 feet long above the water." [22]

The testimony given by Captain John J. Knapp, United States Navy hydrographer, Day Sixteen, Saturday, May 18, 1912, *Titanic* Disaster Hearings was especially descriptive of the ice field that the Titanic apparently ran into on the evening of April 14, 1912. Captain Knapp read several telegrams from other ships, in particular the *S.S. Meeba*,

"April 14, 11 A.M., latitude 41° 50' north, longitude 49° 15' west, passed a quantity of bergs, some very large; also a field of pack ice about 5 miles long. April 14, 2 P.M., 42° north, longitude 50°, passes another field of pack ice with numerous bergs intermixed, and extended from 4 points on the starboard bow to abeam on the

17

port side. Had to steer about 20 miles south to clear it. Ice seemed to be one solid wall of ice at least 16 feet high, as far as could be seen. In latitude 41° 35' north, longitude 50° 30 west, we came to the end of it at 4 PM we were able to again steer to the westward. Saw no more ice after this. Weather clear and bright."[23]

Even after reviewing the above testimony and understanding that even ninety-nine years after the sinking of the *Titanic*, no one has ever conclusively produced direct evidence as to the actual size of the iceberg that sank her. It would only seem logical therefore to assume that any lay person, professional seamen, historian or film director who did not actually see the iceberg, would naturally conclude that since the *Titanic* was the largest passenger ship afloat at that time, any iceberg that sank the mighty ship world almost certainly have to be equally as large and need I say "*Titanic*".

This would explain why Captain Rostron of the *Carpathia,* Captain Knapp, United States Navy hydrographer, Captain Moore of the ship *Mount Temple* all seemed fixated on large icebergs during the hearings thus setting the stage for the urban legend that the *Titanic* was sunk by the mother of all icebergs.

Unfortunately, as revealed by eyewitnesses who saw the actual iceberg on the evening of April 14, 1912, nothing could be further from the truth. The iceberg that sank the mighty *Titanic* was, by all accounts, quite small indeed.

It is also clear that the *Titanic* did not hit a single iceberg that was floating in the frigid Atlantic Ocean, but rather ran into a significant ice flow and ice pack that was congested with icebergs of all sizes ranging from boulders, growlers and small to large icebergs in an area five miles wide by twenty miles long, stretching directly in the path of the speeding ship as shown in the drawing in (Figure One).

Some have suggested that the *Titanic*, in trying to avoid the iceberg that Fleet saw, accidentally struck another iceberg that resulted in the sinking of the mighty ship. The two iceberg theory was suggested in the 1953 *Titanic* film. This theory is somewhat plausible, but in looking at the map in Figure One, it is certainly not groundbreaking.

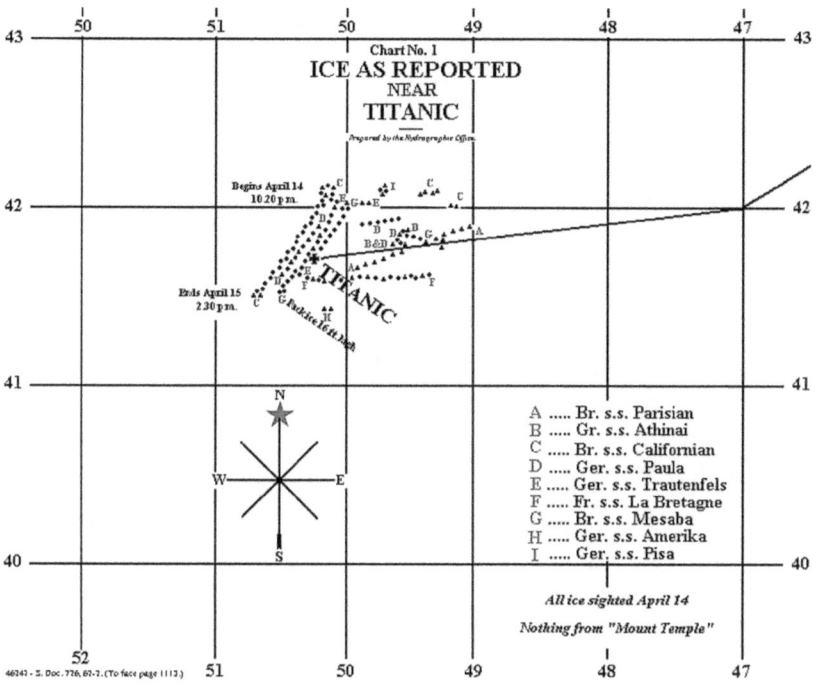

FIGURE ONE[24]

In retrospect, the *Titanic* was not a bowling ball aimed at a single ten pin as described in the beginning of this chapter. Nor was it a bowling ball that missed the ten pin but hit the nine pin instead. Traveling as she was at approximately 22 knots, the *Titanic* was rather like a comet on a collision course with the planet Earth. As she approached the one hundred square mile ice field, the *Titanic* was going to hit something that night and this fact alone made any other outcome, other than her sinking, highly improbable.

CHAPTER THREE
CONTINUOUS GASH THEORY

The *Titanic* "urban legend" blamed a single spur of the iceberg that hit the ship below the waterline and sliced a continuous gash in the hull slightly above the turn of the bilge, flooding six water tight compartments and thus, sinking the *Titanic*. The 1953 film *Titanic*, the 1958 film *A Night To Remember* and the 1997 film *Titanic* all show a massive gash being made in the starboard hull of the *Titanic* flooding compartments one, two, three, four and boiler rooms six and five. Unfortunately, in the 1953 film the film also mistakenly shows the berg piercing the "port" side, not the "starboard" side of the ship.

During the 1912 *Titanic* hearings in the United States and in England, up to and including much of the 1980s, the continuous gash theory was accepted as the gospel truth as to how the ship flooded and was considered to be the only explanation as to why the *Titanic* sank.

However, after the ships wreckage was discovered in 1985, attempts were made using a sonic imaging device, to penetrate the sixty feet of mud that buried the *Titanic's* bow when she hit the muddy bottom of the Atlantic ocean traveling at a speed of approximately 30 knots. It was discovered that six non-continuous openings were visible in the starboard hull and were strategically placed in each of the five watertight compartments that flooded that fateful night. Later on however, it was discovered that there were similar and even more openings along the port side, suggesting that the openings occurred when the *Titanic* hit the ocean floor and were not the result of the iceberg.[25]

It is important therefore that there be a complete understanding of how the *Titanic* was designed before we get into what possibly did occur on the evening of April 14, 1912.

WATER TIGHT COMPARTMENTS

Let us revisit some vital statistics. The *Titanic* was 882 feet 9 inches long and her breadth was 92.5 feet. The height of the boat deck above the waterline at the time of the accident was approximately 58 feet. Her hull displacement at the time of the collision was 34 feet, 7 inches, equaled a displacement of 52,310 tons of water.

Fifteen transverse vertical bulkheads divided the ship into sixteen watertight compartments. Starting at the bow, the bulkheads were labeled "A" through "P". However, all of the watertight compartments did not extend to the top deck "C". Only bulkhead "A" extended to "C" deck, but was only watertight to "D" deck. The other bulkheads ascended upwards to either "D" or "E" deck. [26]

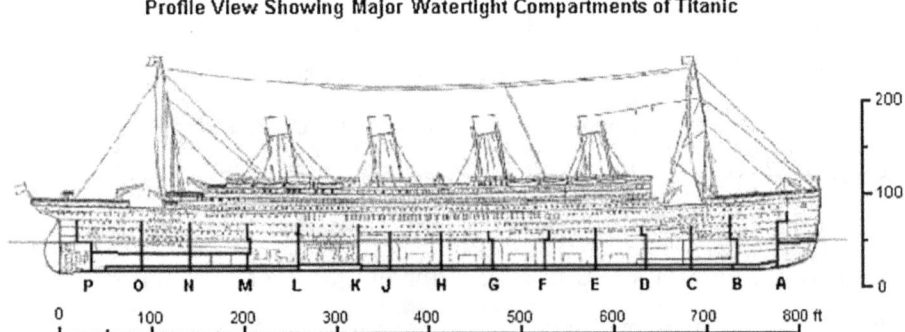

Profile View Showing Major Watertight Compartments of Titanic

FIGURE TWO [27]

The transverse watertight compartments were only watertight vertically and did not have a watertight tank top or watertight top deck. To be truly watertight, each compartment would have had to be watertight on all six sides: port side, starboard side, bow side, stern side, lower and upper tank top side. In the case of the *Titanic*, the compartments were only watertight on five sides, the top was open. Each watertight compartment also had hatchway openings between decks, which allowed water to rise vertically throughout each watertight compartment. Therefore, on the night of the disaster, when the water reached the top of the vertical bulkhead, without a watertight tank top, the water could and did overflow into the next so called "watertight" compartment. This process continued from the bow to the stern until the ship broke apart and sank.

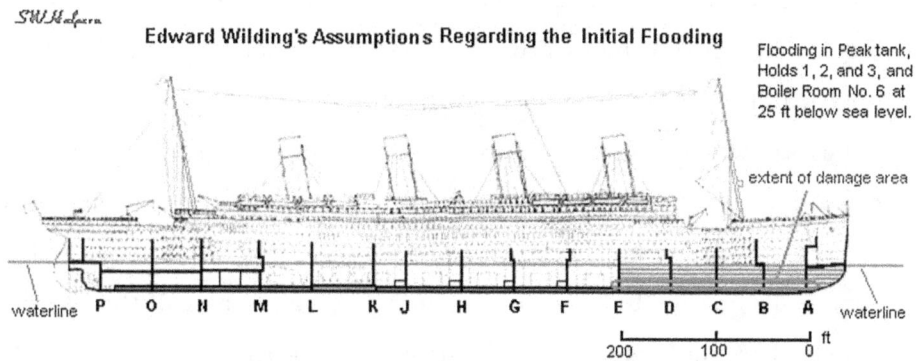

FIGURE 3[28]

It is important to understand the spatial relationship between the decks and the waterline. When the *Titanic* struck the iceberg, the forward part of the ship flooded rapidly and as a result, each deck descended below the waterline.

Because the *Titanic* was tapered upward at the bow, "D" deck stood 33 feet above the waterline, "E" deck stood 24 feet and "F" deck was feet 15 feet 6 inches above the waterline. Amidships however, "D" deck was only 20 feet above the waterline, "E" deck was only 11 feet and "F" deck was only 2 feet above the waterline. Decks that were below the waterline were "G" deck aft and both Orlop decks bow and aft. "G" deck forward was 7 feet 6 inches above the waterline at the moment of impact.[29]

Oddly enough, when the *Titanic* first struck the iceberg, it would have been apparent to anyone walking toward the bow on the Tank Top Deck in Hold #1 that the water inside the ship seemed to be flowing down from the bow heading toward the amidships position and fireman's tunnel, driven not only by the water pressure from outside that was forcing its way into the ship, replacing and venting the air inside the watertight compartment through the hatchway openings mentioned earlier, but the slope of the ship as well. Added to this tsunami, would be the additional force of the water caused by the forward momentum of the ship that was moving forward at approximately 22 knots.

It is known that Harland and Wolff designed the *Titanic* to remain afloat even in the event that any two of the largest compartments were filled with water, their having taken into consideration two types of accidents, a frontal "T-bone" collision with the Titanic being the base of the "T" or a collision where the Titanic would be struck by another ship, thus being the cross of the "T".

Furthermore, even if three of the first four compartments were flooded, the ship would remain afloat since the weight would not bring the ship down far enough by the bow to reach the top of the vertical bulkheads on "E" deck. In fact, even if all four of the forward compartments were flooded, the ship could remain afloat. But unfortunately, this was not to be the case. When, on the night of April 14,1912 Engine Room #6 flooded, the fate of the mighty ship was sealed.[30]

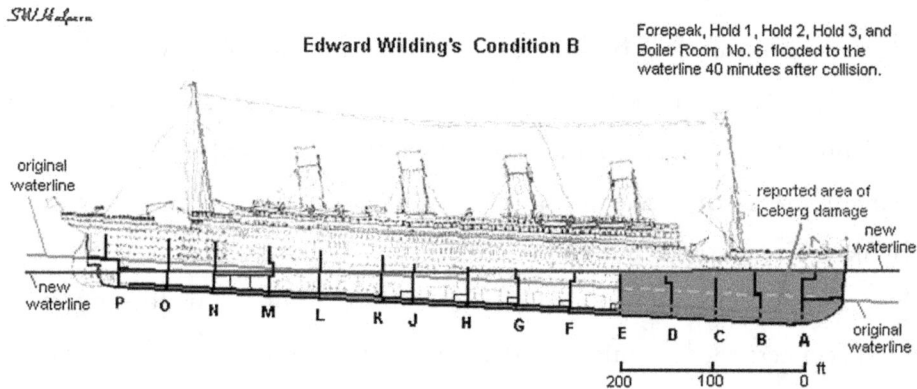

FIGURE 4 [31]

Another point to consider was the ten-day coalbunker fire that heated the watertight bulkhead between Boiler Room #6 and #5. The watertight bulkhead "E" that separated boiler room #6 and #5 also separated the coalbunkers in Boiler room #6 and #5. The coalbunker fire was located in the starboard aft bunker in boiler room #6. The watertight bulkhead "E" was the common wall for the coalbunker for both Boiler Room #6 and #5 where Barrett said he saw water entering the ship. Regarding the heat damage to the bulkhead, stoker Frederick Barrett testified at the British Wreck Commission, *"The bottom of the watertight compartment was dinged aft and the other part was dinged forward."*[32]

There has been a great deal of controversy regarding the exact method used to put out this coalbunker fire. Testimony supports the fact that water was used to wet the coal as the men shoveled the coal from the bunker into the furnace. Many suggest that this was not done because wet coal could spontaneously erupt and the salt water would be harmful to the furnace interior. Others argue that the bunker that Leading Fireman Barrett, Leading Fireman Hendrickson and Fireman Dilley identified was incorrect and that the real bunker fire was in the coalbunker on the starboard front that was connected to bulkhead "D" that separated Boiler Room #6 with Hold #3. These supporters argue that if the bunker fire was indeed in the coal bunker described by Barrett, Hendrickson and Dilley, then the coal bunker fire would have spread to Boiler Room #5 since these two coal bunkers shared the common bulkhead "E", a bulkhead that was cherry red hot from the bunker fire in Boiler Room #6. Following the testimony of all concerned, it would be logical that water was used to keep the fire from spreading and possibly cooling the common bulkhead "E" while both coal bunkers in Boiler Room #6 and Boiler Room #5 were emptied simultaneously as the coal was shoveled into their respective furnaces.

It should be noted that the British Wreck Commission asked Barrett several probing questions implying that the bulkhead between boiler room #6 and #5 did not collapse, but rather there was a collection of water in the "empty" coalbunker in boiler room #5 caused by the collision with the iceberg that opened a two foot seam approximately two feet above the bilge and Barrett when he shut the bunker doors. Since the bunker doors were not watertight, when enough water collected inside of the bunker to force the doors open, it would have burst through giving Barrett the impression that the bulkhead had collapsed as he hurried up the escape latter to safety.

Some have doubted the argument that the water that Barrett saw was the result of the coal bunker doors bursting open from the confined water buildup by point out that there were grates in the bottom of the doors to allow for venting of methane gasses. One has to wonder if the gratings were small enough, or if the water flow was great enough to overcome the escaping water through the gratings. In either case, the doors would have still burst open.

However, if bulkhead "E" was weakened by the heat of the burning coal, could it have possibly added to the circumstances that might have led to the collapse of the bulkhead "E" between boiler room #6 and #5?

This point, however relevant, is "moot" since the *Titanic* could not have remained afloat with the flooding of her first four watertight compartments and boiler room #6 in any event.

All we know for certain regarding the flooding of engine room #6 and the possible collapse of the bulkhead "E" separating Boiler Room #6 & #5 is the testimony of Frederick Barrett at the U.S. Senate hearing,

"*Q: How big was this hole in the side?*

A: About 2 feet above the floor plates, starboard side.

Q: How much water?

A: A large volume of water came through.

Q: How big was this hole in the side?

A: About 2 feet above the floor plates.

Q: You think it was a large tear?

A: Yes I do.

Q: All along the side of No. 6?

A: Yes.

Q: How far along?

A: Past the bulkhead between sections 5 and 6, and it was a hole 2 feet into the coal bunkers. She was torn through No.6 and also through 2 feet abaft the bulkhead in the bunker at the forward head of No. 5 section. We got through before the doors broke, the doors dropped instantly, automatically from the bridge. I went back to No. 6 fireroom and there was 8 feet of water in there. I went to No. 5 fireroom when the lights went out. I was sent to find lamps, as the lights were out, and when we got the lamps we looked at the boilers and there was no water in them. I ran to the engineer and he told me to get some firemen down to draw the fires. I got 15 men down below.

Q: Did you have fires in No.6?

A: Yes. The fires were lit when the water came.

Q: I would like to know how many boilers were going that night?

A: There were five boilers not lit.

Q: How many were there going?

A: There were 24 boilers lit and five without. Fires were lighted in three boilers for the first time Sunday, but I do not know if they were connected or not.

Q: This tear went a couple of feet past the bulkhead in No. 5. How were you able to keep the water from reaching...

A: It never came above the plates, until all at once I saw a wave of green foam come tearing through between the boilers and I jumped for the escape ladder."[33]

THE DOUBLE BOTTOM

There was a little known area of the *Titanic*, referred to as the "hidden deck". Detailed information regarding the "hidden deck" is published on the Internet by Samuel Halpern on April 8, 2005, ET Research, *Titanic's Hidden Deck, An examination of the Titanic's double bottom.* It seems that the *Titanic* was constructed with an inner bottom tank top that was watertight and was separated from the outer skin by a distance of approximately five feet. Unfortunately, the double bottom of the *Titanic* was somewhat like the "watertight" compartments that were not really watertight since the double bottom under the "tank top" deck did not cover the entire bottom.

To quote Mr. Halpern, *"The tank top of the* Titanic *formed a watertight inner bottom about 5 feet above the top of the keel. The extent of the inner bottom was from bulkhead A, the first major watertight transverse bulkhead near the bow, to about 20 ft in front of bulkhead P, the last major watertight transverse bulkhead near the stern. In other words, the inner bottom extended for almost the entire length of the vessel except for a small distance at each end. The inner bottom was also subdivided by a watertight center keelson extending 670 ft from bulkhead B to bulkhead O, and two watertight longitudinal bulkheads located* for the most part about 30 ft. from the center line amidships and extending 447 ft from bulkhead D to bulkhead M. Thus, between transverse bulkheads D and M, with the exception of the reciprocating engine room, each compartment had a cellular double bottom that was divided into four tanks, one tank to port and another to starboard of the center keelson, and two wing tanks, one on the port side and the other on the starboard side. Under the reciprocating engine room, there were also two wing tanks, but on each side of the center keelson there were two tanks, 2 on the port side and 2 on the starboard side. This was created by a watertight transverse division under the center of the reciprocating engine room that extended out to inner sides of the wing tanks. Between bulkheads B and D and between bulkheads M and O, there was the watertight division at the center keelson only, forming two tanks under each major compartment there. Between bulkheads A and B and aft of bulkhead O to 20 feet before bulkhead P, there was only one tank under each compartment.

    The Titanic was constructed with a double bottom keel. The outer keel was separated by five feet from the inner tank top and was water proof. Unfortunately, the entire keel of the Titanic was not a double bottom. Sections of the bow and the stern were not double bottomed but only had a single bottom as did the vertical side of the hull." [34]

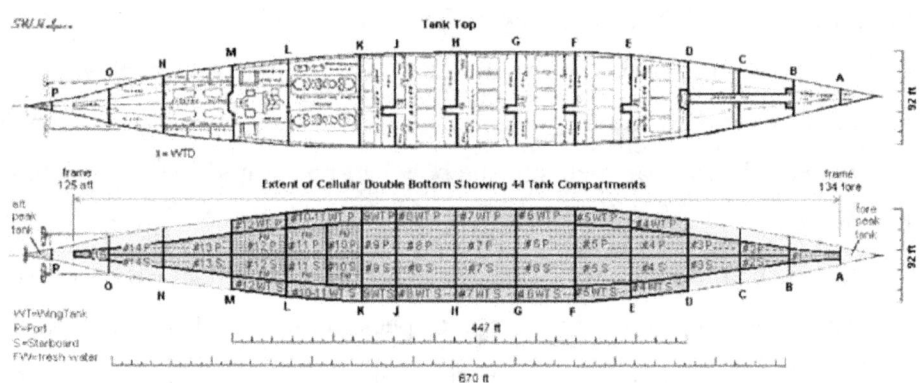

FIGURE FIVE [35]

Considering the statements made by Mr. Halpern and viewing the *Titanic's* hidden deck in Fig. 5, it is quite clear that the only thing that separated the sea from the inner decks of the ship in the bow and stern sections were only one inch thick steel plates. There was no double bottom in these areas.

Furthermore, although the double bottom design did not extend up the side walls of the *Titanic's* hull from Bulkhead "D" to "M", there were "wing" tanks in the hidden deck that did follow the curve of the bilge extending seven feet above the keel, or two feet above the floor of the "tank top".

According to Mr. Halpern, the double bottom contained, "*46 watertight compartments in the ship's bottom, 44 within the cellular double bottom, plus the fore and aft peak tanks 44 tanks that were designed to carry salt water for ballast. Some of the tanks could do double duty and carry either fresh or salt water. The total water ballast capacity of these tanks, including the peak tanks and those used for fresh water only, was 5754 tons*" [36]

The important point to remember about the cellular double bottom is that it did not extend across the entire bottom, port to starboard, from bulkhead "A" to "D" at the bow and bulkheads "M" through "P" at the stern. To be more specific, from bulkhead "A" trough "D", there was only one tank under each watertight compartment, which means that the first four watertight compartments in the bow had no complete cellular double bottom.

It is also important to understand that at the bow and stern of the *Titanic*, there were massive watertight "peek" tanks filled with salt water for ballast that was used to "trim" the ship. These peek tanks extended up to the Orlop deck in the bow's fore peek tank and to deck G in the stern aft peek tank. Both tanks were watertight on the top, thus creating the floor for the Orlop deck in the bow and "G" deck in the stern.

Interestingly enough, there was no cellular wall for these peek tanks, which instead, used the hull of the ship as their sidewalls. Holds one, two and three also did not have complete cellular bottom tank top, making the starboard bow the weakest part of the ship, aptly described as its Achilles heel. Unfortunately, it was here, that the mighty *Titanic* hit the iceberg.

CHAPTER 4
STEAM BOILERS AND ELECTRICITY

In 1912, the primary source of energy was steam, steam and more steam and therefore it was only to be expected that steam power was used to propel the ocean liners and freighters that crossed the seven seas. The *Titanic* had 24 double – ended Scotch boilers and five single-ended auxiliary boilers. The five single ended boilers were used to provide steam to the electric dynamos that provided electricity to the ship and were located in Boiler Room #1. The electricity was produced by four 400 Kilowatt electric generators that produced 16,000 A at 100V. There were also two emergency 30 Kilowatt generators on D Deck. It is important to note that steam at a pressure of 185 pounds per square inch was required to power the 400 Kilowatt generators.[37] It is also important to note at this time that Boiler Room #1 was never used on the maiden voyage simply because there was no coal loaded into the coal bunkers due to the coal strike which resulted in a critical coal shortage for the entire shipping industry.

In Samuel Halpern's Monday 9 July 2007 paper for the Encyclopedia Titanica, *Titanic's Prime Mover – An Examination of Propulsion and Power, Auxiliary Steam Supply and the Electrical Power Plant*, Halpern states that, "*The ship had four main electric dynamos with a capacity of 400 kilowatts each. They produced 100v direct current (DC). These dynamos, and the steam engines that drove them, were situated in a separate watertight compartment located aft of the turbine room. The 580 indicated horsepower steam engine drove each dynamo were vertical, three-crank, compound engines with one HP and two LP Cylinders.*

They ran at 325 revolutions per minute, and took in steam at 185 psig from two separate steam supply pipes to which they could be cross connected. One pipe was on the port side and was connected to five single-ended boilers in BR No. 1 and with two port –side double ended boilers in BR No. 2. The other supply pipe, on the starboard side, was the auxiliary steam supply that was connected to the five single-ended boilers in BR No. 1 and to the two port-side double-ended boilers in No. 2, and the two starboard-side double ended boilers in No. 4.

In addition to these, there was a separate steam pipe leading to a pair of emergency dynamo engines situated on a platform 20 feet above the ship's waterline on D Deck on the aft side of the turbine engine room casing. These emergency dynamos produced 30 kilowatts of electric power each at 100 volts DC. These sets supplied power to 500 incandescent lamps fitted throughout all passenger and machinery compartments, at the end of passages, near stairways, and on the Boat deck. There were also change-over switches that enabled 5 arc lamps, 7 cargo and gangway lamps, the ships navigation lights, the lights on the navigation bridge (including the wheelhouse and chart rooms), the Marconi apparatus, and 4 electrically-driven boat winches all to be connected up to the emergency circuit if needed. It was a practice to run these emergency dynamos every night after sunset in case of an accident to the main electrical supply during the night.

Each emergency dynamo was driven at 380 revolutions per minute by a two-crank, compound engine with one HP and one LP cylinders. The emergency steam supply pipe that fed these engines ran along E deck above the watertight bulkheads and was arranged so it can take steam from the double-ended boilers in any of the three boiler rooms No. 2, 3, or 5. As a backup in case of accident to the main steam supply pipes, there was a connection that branched off this emergency supply pipe to the pumps in the engine room that were connected to the bilges throughout the ship. There was also a cross connection to this pipe so that the steam reaching the engine room from any boiler in the ship could be passed up to the emergency dynamos by opening two or three valves." [38]

Many of the survivors told the United States and British investigating committees that the lights remained on right to the end when the *Titanic* took her final plunge, for example Archie Jewell, Look Out on the *Titanic* testified at the British Wreck Commissioner's Inquiry as follows:

" *175 -Just tell us shortly what you yourself saw then. What did you see that happened to the "Titanic" before she went down and as she went down?*

- We stopped there and watched her gradually sink away. We could see the people about on the deck before the lights went out. As she went away by the head so the lights went out, and we heard some explosions as she was going down. But all the lights went out and we could only see a black object in front of us."[39]

Other accounts include the following:

British Wreck Commissioner's Inquiry, testimony from Albert V. Pearcey, third class pantryman,

"*10454. Were her lights burning?*

- Yes, the lights were burning.

10455. Up to the last?

- Yes

10456. Can you give us any idea of how long it was after you had started rowing away from the "Titanic" before she sank?

- No, I cannot. It was 20 minutes to two when we came away from her."

United States Senate Inquiry, Alfred Olliver, Quartermaster of the *Titanic*, United States Senate Inquiry testified that:

"*Senator BURTON.*

Did you see the boat sink?

Mr. OLLIVER.

I can not say that I saw it right plain; but to my imagination I did, because the lights went out before she went down." [40]

The testimony given above by these men and that of other survivors is critical in understanding the events that led up to the sinking of the *Titanic*.

The electric lights that were burning in the darkness of the Atlantic on the morning of April 15, 1912 were made possible by the steam which powered the electric generators at a pressure of 185 psig which in turn produced the electricity that lit the electric lights. Therefore, it is a simple matter to deduce that some of the boilers were still fired since boiler rooms 4, 3, 2 and 1 were untouched by the iceberg; however, Boiler Room #1 was not used during the duration of the voyage and Boiler Room 4 started to flood at the end, approximately one hour and five minutes before the ship sank. This would leave regular and emergency steam lines that ran from Boiler Rooms #3 and #2 to power the dynamos. It is obvious that some of the boilers had to have steam in them up to the moment that the Titanic made its final plunge. If this had not been so, there simply would have been no electric lights prior to and up to the sinking. When the time came for the *Titanic* to disappear forever beneath the surface of the Atlantic Ocean, the working boilers flooded, exploded and the steam they were producing stopped flowing. When that happened, the dynamos ceased functioning and the lights on the *Titanic* went out forever.

CHAPTER 5
LISTING TO PORT

The "urban legend" and Hollywood do not really say very much about the direction in which the *Titanic* was listing after she hit the iceberg. However, there is a great deal of testimony about this important issue that should be reviewed if we are to understand what actually happened that fateful night.

When the *Titanic* first hit the iceberg, Captain Smith checked the commutator, a simple pendulum device, and noted that the *Titanic* was listing 5 ° starboards as reported by Mr. Hitchenes at the United States Titanic Disaster Hearings. Mr. Hitchenes, the *Titanic's* Helsman who was, at the wheel when the iceberg struck testified:

"Capt. Smith, sir, to Mr. Murdoch; ' Close the emergency doors.' Mr. Murdoch replied, 'The doors are already closed.' The captain sent then for the carpenter to sound the ship. He also came back to the wheelhouse and looked at the commentator in front of the compass, which is a little instrument like a clock to tell you how the ship is listing. The ship had a list of 5° to the starboard."[41]

This was verified by Mr. George A Harder, Brooklyn manufacturer and first class passenger, who testified at the United States Titanic Disaster Hearings, "I walked around the deck two or three times, when I noticed that the boat was listing quite a good deal on the starboard side."[42]

And a Seaman on the *Titanic*, a certain Frank Osman, testified at the United States Titanic Disaster Hearings that the ship was listing four to five degrees to the starboard. [43]

However, as the bow of the ship sank lower and lower, the *Titanic* actually listed toward the port side to such a degree that many passengers had to jump across an ever widening gap on the port side in order to get into the lifeboats, as did First Class passenger Hugh Woolner who testified on Day 10 at the American *Titanic* Disaster Hearings,

"*Senator SMITH.*

You remained down there with your friend until the sea came in - water came in - on A deck?

Mr. WOOLNER.

On that A deck. Then we hopped up onto the gunwale preparing to jump out into the sea, because if we had waited a minute longer we should have been boxed in against the ceiling. And as we looked out we saw this collapsible, the last boat on the port side, being lowered right in front of our faces.

Senator SMITH.

How far out?

Mr. WOOLNER.

It was about 9 feet out?

Senator SMITH.

Nine feet out from the side of A deck?

Mr. WOOLNER.

Yes." [44]

Those on the starboard side, had to push the lifeboat away from the hull of the Titanic to be lowered into the water as explained by George T. Rowe, Q.M., who was sworn in by Senator Burton at the United States hearings on day seven,

"*Senator BURTON.*

Was the Titanic down by the head?

Mr. ROWE.

Yes, sir. When we left the ship the fore-well deck was awash; that is, when we pushed off from the ship. It was 1.25 when I left the bridge to get into the boat.

When the boat was in the water the well deck was submerged. It took us a good five minutes to lower the boat on account of this rubbing going down." [45]

There is a fascinating twenty-one minute tape of Ms. Edith Russell's audio account of how she was thrown into the lifeboat, having been unable to jump because of her tight skirt, available on the Internet. This account can be heard at http://www.bbc.co.uk/archive/titanic/5051.shtml.

The Titanic "urban legend" reports that the *Titanic* hit the iceberg with a glancing blow and the iceberg cut a continuous 300 foot long gash in her starboard side, even though testimony at the 1912 British Wreck Commissioner's Inquiry by Edward Wilding, a Harland and Wolff employee, strongly suggested that there were instead multiple areas of damage.

"20422. There is one other thing I think you wanted to tell us upon the points you have left. Have you made any calculation as to the volume of water that came in through the apertures of this vessel?

- Yes. I referred this to this condition B on the plan I put in, and corresponding very nearly to condition D on the third plan. Assuming the forepeak and Nos. 1, 2 and 3 holds and No. 6 boiler room flooded, and that the water has risen to the waterline which is shown on those diagrams, it would mean that about 16,000 tons of water had found their way into the vessel. That is the volume of the water which would have to come in. As far as I can follow from the evidence, the water was up to that level in about 40 minutes. It may be a few minutes more or less, but that was the best estimate I could make. When the inflow started the evidence we have as to the vertical position of the damage indicated that the head would be about 25 feet. Of course, as the water rose inside, that head would be reduced and the rate of inflow would be reduced somewhat. Making allowance for those, My estimate for the size of the hole required (and making some allowance for the obstruction due to the presence of decks and other things.), is that the total area through which water was entering the ship, was somewhere about 12 square feet. The extent of the damage fore and

aft, that is from the foremost puncture to the aftermost puncture in the cross bunker at the forward end of No. 5 boiler room, is about 500 feet, and the average width of the hole extending the whole way is only about three-quarters of an inch. That was my reason for stating this morning that I believe it must have been in places, that is, not a continuous rip. A hole three-quarters of an inch wide and 200 feet long does not seem to describe to me the probable damage, but it must have averaged about that amount."[46]

However, since 1985 with the Dr. Ballard's discovery of the *Titanic*, the "urban legend" has shifted somewhat to describe a glancing blow to the side of the *Titanic* that was much like a rubber paddle ball bouncing across the hull of the *Titanic*, thus making several non-continuous gashes in the hull that extended from the bow to boiler room #5. As a result of the immediate flooding of the lower decks, the *Titanic* initially began to list starboard and yet as the drama unfolded, the Titanic listed to the port side. Why?

As described in Chapter 3, the *Titanic* had a "hidden deck" that contained forty-four watertight compartments within the cellular double bottom of the ship. These compartments were used for storage of boiler water, fresh water as well as to provide ballast. Ballast on ships was not a new technology in 1912. In fact, as early as 1849, President Lincoln had filed for a patent that described a water ballast system that would allow for a ship to pass over shoals in rivers.

With this in mind, it is essential to consider the possible events that may have caused the list to port.

STARTING UP ENGINES

The Titanic struck an iceberg and immediately listed to starboard. After a short while, the ship started moving again as described an affidavit that was filed with the United States Titanic Disaster Hearings by Mrs. Mahala D. Douglas, of Minneapolis, MN, First Class passenger. Mrs. Douglas states that the Titanic, after stopping its engines, resumed steaming, *"The shock of the collision was not great to us; the engines stopped, then went on for a few moments, then stopped again."*[47]

Greaser Frederick Scott testified at the British Titanic Wreak hearings as follows,

"5522. We know it was about 11.40?

- Yes, about 20 minutes to 12.

5523. Did you notice the two telegraphs in the engine room?

- Yes; four telegraphs rang.

5524. Were there four telegraphs?

- She got four telegraphs, two emergency ones.

5525. Two emergency?

- Yes, and two for the main engine.

5526. What did you notice?

- I noticed "Stop" first.

5527. To which telegraph did that come?

- On the main engines.

5528. Let us get this clearly. I understand you are speaking now of the turbine room?

- No, there are two stand-bys; you can see just the same in the turbine room; if you are standing at the engine room door you can see the two just the same.

5529. Where did you see those?

- In the main engine room.

5530. That is where the reciprocating engines are?

- Yes.

5531. The watertight door is open?

- Yes.

5532. And you can see through?

- Yes.

5533. Now I think we follow. When you speak of the four telegraphs, are they all there?

- Yes.

5534. Or are there any in your room?

- No, there are none in the turbine room at all, Sir, all in the main engine room.

5535. Was the telegraph signal that came the emergency or the ordinary telegraph?

- That is to the main engine room. It is different. They ring the two on the main engine room, and then they ring two others just afterwards, the emergency ones.

5536. Did you hear the two?

- All four went.

5537. Did you hear the two ordinary ones ring first?

- No, they all four rang together.

5538. What did they ring?

- "Stop."

5539. Was that before or after the shock?

- After the shock.

5540. What was the next thing?

- Then the watertight doors went.

5541. Was any reply given to the telegraph orders from the bridge?

- Yes, they rang back from the engine room; the two greasers at the bottom rang back.

5542. It would be their duty, I suppose, to ring back?

- Yes.

5543. Did you see them do that?

- Yes.

5544. After they got the order to stop?

- Yes, they were feeding the engines, and were close handy at the time.

5545. *They happened to be there?*

- Yes.

5546. *Then the next thing that happened was something with reference to the watertight doors?*

- Yes, the watertight doors all closed.

5547. *Did you hear any bell ring first?*

- No, not for the watertight doors.

5548. *Do you mean that without any signal they came down?*

- Yes.

5549. *Which watertight doors are you speaking of?*

- All of them.

5550. *When you say "all of them," how many do you mean?*

- I think it is about six, leading down to the afterend of the tunnel.

5551. *Do you mean not only in your engine room, but you are speaking also of what you could see aft; the other watertight doors had been open?*

- We had to go and open them up afterwards.

5552. *I understand now what you mean. You are standing in the turbine engine room and there you have got watertight doors fore and aft which were open, and aft you could see the other watertight doors were open?*

- Yes.

5553. *Then, if I follow you correctly, what happened was, all those doors closed down at the same time?*

- Yes.

5554. *What did you do after that?*

- After that we went up to the turbine room and down one of the escapes to let one of the greasers out in the after tunnel.

5555. *That is into the electric room?*

- No, there is another tunnel after that one.

5556. Do you mean the aftermost one?

- Yes, the aftermost one of the lot.

5557. That is the very last on the tank top, your Lordship will see. (To the Witness.) You went there?

- Yes, and heaved the door up about two feet to let the greaser out.

5558. Who was the greaser there?

- He was tunnel greaser, the one who looks after the tunnel.

5559. You had to release him?

- We had to go and heave the door up.

5560. How many did it take to heave the door up?

- Two of us.

5561. That you did by winding it up, I suppose?

- Yes.

5562. Did you have to give any signal before that?

- No.

5563. Did you get any order?

- No.

5564. Did you do it by yourselves?

- Yes, me and my mate on the other side of the engine room.

5565. Did you hear any signal given to the bridge?

- From the engine room?

5566. Yes?

- Yes.

5567. What?

- When they rang the stand-by. Is that what you mean?

5568. Yes?

- That is all I heard, and then they rang down, "Slow Ahead!" [48]

It is clear that after striking the iceberg the *Titanic's* stopped her engines and the, for some inexplicable reason, started them up again. Samuel

Halpern states in his Internet paper, *Somewhere About 12 Square Feet*, "*There has been much speculation as to why the ship would be moved ahead again after the collision, including the possibility that they needed to get clear of some nearby ice so that lifeboats could be launched safely.*"[49] Unfortunately, it would seem that the steaming forward preceded the realization that the ship was severely damaged and the uncovering of the lifeboats. This riddle will never be completely solved since Captain Smith died that faithful night and everyone else who was in charge of the Titanic either perished with him or died a natural death years later. But this is what might possibly have happened.

Consider this, it is entirely possible that the ship listed portside because it was flooding from the starboard side, it being only logical to assume that, before restarting the engines, Captain Smith would have flooded her port ballast tanks to stop the starboard list. After doing that, he may have decided to steam forward at "Slow Ahead" for several minutes until he realized the severity of the damage and stopped the engines for the last time. This argument was addressed at the British Wreck Commissioner's Inquiry,

"*The Commissioner:*

Perhaps it is in the evidence and I have overlooked it; but I have not yet understood what the cause of this list to port was.

The Attorney-General:

I agree it is very difficult to understand. Mr. Wilding has a view about it, and he might answer it at once.

20229. (The Commissioner.) Wait a moment. It is suggested to me that perhaps the list in the "Titanic" was very much smaller than the list which would be caused by one of the "Mauretania's" side bunkers being flooded. Is that so?

- Probably, My Lord.

20230. (Mr. Rowlatt.) Can you, to any extent, counteract the flooding, we will say, of one of the bunkers on the side of a ship like the "Mauretania" by letting

in water to the double bottom on the other side of the ship, for a greater length of the ship, at the extreme wing of the double bottom? That has been suggested, you know.

- I quite understand the point, but the available arrangements, the pipe arrangements for flooding any bottom space, act comparatively slowly, and it would therefore take in the first place a long time to correct the list.

20231. But suppose, instead of flooding these spaces on the bottom of the ship, you were to flood a corresponding coal bunker on the other side?

- It would be very difficult to keep flooding arrangements in a bunker in good working order. It might be done, but it would not be easy. The same objection applies as to working the watertight doors. Coal dust chokes up the working of them; it is a practical difficulty, My Lord." [50]

The interesting point to consider here is that, if Captain Smith really thought it necessary to trim the ship, would he have done so by flooding the ballast? More importantly is the question; did he have the time to do this? The answer is probably not.

When the *Titanic* first hit the iceberg, there was considerable confusion. The watertight doors were closed and Captain Smith arrived at the bridge where he was given details of the situation by his officers. Listen to Fourth Officer Boxhall as he testified at the United States Titanic Disaster Hearings on Day Three that,

"*Senator SMITH.*

After these signals were turned in, what was done?

Mr. BOXHALL.

I do not know what was done, because I left the bridge then.

Senator SMITH.

Where did you go?

Mr. BOXHALL.

I went right down below, in the lowest steerage, as far as I could possibly get without going into the cargo portion of the ship, and inspected all the decks as I came up, in the vicinity of where I thought she had struck.

Senator SMITH.

What did you find?

Mr. BOXHALL.

I found no damage. I found no indications to show that the ship had damaged herself.

Senator SMITH.

On the inside?

Mr. BOXHALL.

On the inside.

Senator SMITH.

Did you say you went to the steerage?

Mr. BOXHALL.

I went down to the steerage.

Senator SMITH.

But found no evidence of injury there?

Mr. BOXHALL.

No, sir.

Senator SMITH.

Then where did you go?

Mr. BOXHALL.

Then I went on the bridge and reported to the captain that I could not see any damage.

Senator SMITH.

One moment. Did you look farther, beyond the steerage?

Mr. BOXHALL.

> *I looked in all the decks. I worked my way up to the top deck.*
>
> Senator SMITH.
>
> *Looking at all of them in the forward part?*
>
> Mr. BOXHALL.
>
> *In the forward part of the ship; that is, abreast of No. 2 and 3 hatches.*
>
> Senator SMITH.
>
> *Then what did you do?*
>
> Mr. BOXHALL.
>
> *I came right up to the bridge and reported that I could find no damage"* [51]

According to David G. Brown in his book, *The Last Log of the TITANIC*, there was a mysterious Marconigram possibly sent by Captain Smith saying that the although the *Titanic* had struck an iceberg, everyone was safe and they were steaming for Halifax.[52] If Captain Smith was indeed the author of this mysterious Marconigram as Mr. Brown suggest, this would explain that he started the *Titanic* steaming at "Slow Ahead" after hitting the iceberg because he honestly thought that the *Titanic* was not severely damaged, in which case his immediate mission would have been to get his passengers and crew to a safe harbor. Could it be that Mr. Boxhall's report to Captain Smith that he had seen no damage could have momentarily convinced Captain Smith that it was safe to start the engines and proceed to Halifax? Possibly, but Captain Smith was a seasoned Master and would have looked for more evidence that the ship was safe to move.

Ismay, in his testimony at the United States Senate Inquiry testified that he spoke with Chief Engineer Bell and was told that the ship had struck ice but the pumps would keep the *Titanic* afloat. After hearing this, Ismay went to the bridge to report to Captain Smith. If Captain Smith first hearing from Fourth Officer Boxhall that the ship was not damaged and then hearing conflicting information from Ismay that there was damage, but the pumps could deal with the situation, Captain Smith may have decided it was safe to steam forward and did so until he understood the full extent of the damage.

After the engines were stopped for the last time, the *Titanic* continued to sink by the bow and drifted with the currents. Now, she would naturally take on a list to port, if her port ballast tanks were indeed flooded. After the engines were stopped for the final time, Captain Smith, preoccupied with launching the lifeboats would have forgotten about the flooded ballast tanks. If he did flood the port ballast tanks, one can only speculate what might have happened if he had thought to blown air into the port ballast tanks after he stopped the ship for the final time. One thing is for certain, unnecessary tons of water inside the ballast tanks could only have hastened the sinking of the mighty *Titanic*.

Another explanation for the list to port was explored by Mr. Edwards at the British Wreck Commission Inquiry who suggested that Captain Smith had instructed that the side gangway doors be opened to allow for the passengers to be loaded onto the partially filled life boats. This he concluded might have caused the sudden list to port,

"Mr. Edwards:

May I recall to your Lordship's mind Mr. Lightoller's instruction was, when they were lowering boat 6, that the boatswain and certain men were to go down and open these gangway doors, his view, as he expressed it, being that certain of the boats should come back when they saw the light and take away certain passengers from them?

- So far as my questions were addressed to him they were simply to ascertain his view as to whether if the gangway doors had been opened forward -

The Commissioner:

Forward?

Mr. Edwards:

Yes, forward. He gave the order both forward and aft, and my questions were addressed to him to show whether, in his view, if at the stage when the order was given in fact the gangway door forward was opened on the port side, that might not have accounted for a big rush of water and a sudden list to port.

20479. (The Commissioner.) *I do not remember that; it has escaped me.* (To the witness.) *What do you say to that?*

- Mr. Lightoller did not convey to my mind that he had given any very distinct order, that is any order that made itself clear which door was intended; but there was evidence that the boats were told to go round to the after door which was the door where this accommodation ladder was provided, and which would be the natural door to go to.

20480. (Mr. Rowlatt.) *Is there any ladder for the forward door?*

- There is none.

20481. *If they had gone there and the ladder had been shipped could people have gone down the ladder and stepped into the boats?*

- Very easily. It is like a yacht or warship accommodation ladder." [53]

After the collision, perhaps the first fatal mistake made by Captain Smith was to continue to steam forward after the *Titanic* struck the iceberg with a hole in the bow. Just as there are many things about what happened that night that we will never know, no one can be certain if he trimmed the ship before he steamed forward. Regardless of whether or not Captain Smith trimmed the damaged ship, even at "Slow Ahead", approximately 8 knots, with a gaping hole in the bow, the force of the forward motion of the ship would have forced unnecessary water into the *Titanic* at a much faster rate and with more pressure than it would normally be the case if she had remained stationary.

The view that if the *Titanic* would have steamed forward, massive amounts of water would be forced into the ship was discredited by Samuel Halpern in his Internet paper *"Somewhere About 12 Square Feet"*, "The bottom line in all of this is that the forward movement of the Titanic that took place after the initial stopping of the vessel could not have significantly contributed very much *to the overall flooding situation if the movement did not continue for any significant length of time at any appreciable speed."* [54]

It should be noted, however, that Mr. Halpern's calculations are based on the "twelve square foot" crack theory that was originally proposed by Edward Wilding at the British Inquiry in 1912 and not the possibility that the removal of a large section of the starboard bow and bottom would have produced a gaping hole through which the water could have been forced into.

As we know, a lot of facts have been uncovered since 1912, for example the fact that the Titanic did indeed break in half, a fact rejected by the British Inquiry. Mr. Wilding's testimony that a twelve square foot hole area was all that would be necessary to sink the *Titanic*, although mathematically sound, has never been proven with any physical evidence at the wreck site. Granted there is sonic imagery evidence that indicate several cracks along the ships starboard side suggesting possible ice damage done to the *Titanic* by the iceberg and support for Mr. Wilding's theory. However, other sonic images show that there are also more cracks present on the port bow below the water line where there was no iceberg damage, suggesting therefore that when the *Titanic's* bow smashed into the mud at 30 knots, she fractured her hull on both sides. [55]

To assume that Mr. Wilding's twelve square foot hole crack theory in regards to the *Titanic's* demise is in fact the "holy word and gospel" is pure nonsense. All Mr. Wilding was doing was an academic exercise for the British Inquiry. In today's vernacular, we would call it a Scientific Wild Ass Guess or SWAG heavily dependent, as it was, on the testimony of some of the survivors and the decisions by the members of the American and British inquiry as to which witnesses they would believe.

It is unfortunate therefore that Hollywood and others have used this twelve square foot hole crack theory over the years to brainwash everyone into believing that this is the only way the *Titanic* could sink within the allotted time of just two hours and forty minutes. Fortunately however, others have dared to poke holes into the current "gospel" and have dared to suggested new theories in the hopes of illuminating the darkness that has shrouded the Titanic for the last ninety-nine years.

Let us consider Captain Smith's possible second error which would have been to open the port side gangway doors once he had stopped for the final time, thereby allowing for water to enter the port side of the ship. An interesting point to keep in mind is that the gangway doors were larger than the proposed 3' by 4', 12 square-foot opening, that Edward Wilding calculated that sank the ship. Captain Smith was aware that the ship was listing to starboard. Therefore, he would have had to have opened the port side gangway doors and directed the lifeboats to be taken there in order to board more passengers. But in so doing, he would have inadvertently opened the ship to another massive influx of water. Even though these doors would not span the five water tight compartments as did the crack proposed by Mr. Wilding, they would have certainly allowed for massive amounts of water to fill the ship above E Deck, thus allowing for the ship to list to port and contributing to the rapidity with which it sank.

Regardless of what Captain Smith did or did not do, the *Titanic* was doomed when Boiler Room #6 flooded, guaranteeing that, sooner or later, the ship would flounder. The unfortunate circumstance was that she floundered sooner rather than later.

CHAPTER 6
POINT OF CONTACT

The "urban legend" really does not go into the flooding of the watertight compartments in any great detail. In Hollywood films, we only see dramatic images of the water flooding the holds and the boiler room, but other than that, the legend and films have little to say on this subject.

It is clear from the testimony given at the American Disaster Hearings and the British Wreck Commissioner's Inquiry that there was a lot more than was first thought going on at the time of the collision with the iceberg and shortly thereafter. On the fourth day of the US Inquiry, testimony from Frederick Fleet, the lookout in the crow's nest on the night of April 14, 1912 pointed out the exact point at which where the *Titanic* struck the iceberg:

"*Senator SMITH.*

But you saw the course altered? And the iceberg struck the ship at what point?

Mr. FLEET.

On the starboard bow, just before the foremast.

Senator SMITH.

How far would that be from the bow's end?

Mr. FLEET.

From the stem?

Senator SMITH.

From the stem.

Mr. FLEET.

About 20 feet.

Senator SMITH.

About 20 feet back from the stem?

Mr. FLEET.

From the stem to where she hit." [56]

Mr. Fleet was in the crow's nest, from the vantage point of which he had a clear view of everything that was happening.

Bruce Ismay said at the American Titanic Disaster Hearing on Day One testified that:

"*Senator NEWLANDS.*

How did the ship strike the iceberg?

Mr. ISMAY.

From information I have received, I think she struck the iceberg a glancing blow between the end of the forecastle and the captain's bridge, just aft of the foremast, sir." [57]

Mr. Boxhall, Fourth Officer testified at the American Titanic Disaster Hearings on Day Three that:

"*Senator SMITH.*

Do you know whether it struck the bow squarely?

Mr. BOXHALL.

It seemed to me to strike the bluff of the bow.

Senator SMITH.

Describe that.

Mr. BOXHALL.

It is in the forward part of the ship, but almost on the side.

Senator SMITH.

On which side?

Mr. BOXHALL.

It is just where the ship begins to widen out on the starboard side.

Senator SMITH.

How far would that be from the front of the ship?

Mr. BOXHALL.

I do not know.

Senator SMITH.

About how far?

Mr. BOXHALL.

I could not say in feet.

Senator SMITH.

How far would it be from the eyes?

Mr. BOXHALL.

I do not know. I could not say.

Senator SMITH.

You could not describe that?

Mr. BOXHALL.

No; you could measure it on the plans, though.

Senator SMITH.

About how far?

Mr. BOXHALL.

I could not say how many feet. I have no idea of the number of feet.

Senator SMITH.

But it was not a square blow on the bow of the ship?

Mr. BOXHALL.

No, sir.

Senator SMITH.

In ordinary parlance, would it be a glancing blow?

Mr. BOXHALL.

A glancing blow." [58]

Major Author. G. Peuchen, First class passenger testified at the American Titanic Disaster Hearings on day four that,

"Senator SMITH.

No; not exactly the same thing. Where was this impact on the bow of the ship?

Maj. PEUCHEN.

It was aft of the bow about 40 feet, I should imagine, on the starboard side - about 40 or 50 feet, I should imagine from where the ice started to come off the iceberg." [59]

Frederick Barrett, Fireman in boiler room #6 testified at the American Titanic Disaster Hearings, Day 18 that,

"Q. You were a fireman on the Titanic? - A. I was leading fireman.

Q. Were you on duty on the night of the accident? - A. Yes.

Q. Where? - A. In 6 section.

Q. Were you there when the accident occurred? - A. Yes. I was standing talking to the second engineer. The bell rang, the red light showed. We sang out shut the doors (indicating the ash doors to the furnaces) and there was a crash just as we sung out. The water came through the ship's side. The engineer and I jumped to the next section. The next section to the forward section is No. 5.

Q. Where did the water come through? - A. About 2 feet above the floor plates, starboard side.

Q. How much water? - A. A large volume of water came through" [60]

Fourth Officer Boxhall testified at the American Titanic Disaster Hearings that,

"Senator SMITH.

What did the captain say?

Mr. BOXHALL.

He said, "Go down and find the carpenter and get him to sound the ship."

Senator SMITH.

Did you do so?

Mr. BOXHALL.

I was proceeding down, but I met the carpenter. {J. Maxwell or J. Hutchinson}

Senator SMITH.

What did you say to him?

Mr. BOXHALL.

I said, "The captain wants you to sound the ship." He said, "The ship is making water," and he went on the bridge to the captain, and I thought I would go down forward again and investigate; and then I met a mail clerk, a man named Smith, and he asked where the captain was. I said, "He is on the bridge." He said, "The mail hold is full" or "filling rapidly." I said, "Well, you go and report it to the captain and I will go down and see," and I proceeded right down into the mail room.

Senator SMITH.

What did you find there?

Mr. BOXHALL.

I went down as far as the sorting room deck and found mail clerks down there working.

Senator SMITH.

Doing what?

Mr. BOXHALL.

Taking letters out of the racks, they seemed to me to be doing.

Senator SMITH.

Taking letters out of the racks and putting them into pouches?

Mr. BOXHALL.

I could not see what they were putting them in.

Senator SMITH.

You could not see what disposition they were making of them?

Mr. BOXHALL.

I looked through an open door and saw these men working at the racks, and directly beneath me was the mail hold, and the water seemed to be then within 2 feet of the deck we were standing on.

Senator SMITH.

What did you do in that situation?

Mr. BOXHALL. (continuing)

And bags of mail floating about. I went right on the bridge again and reported to the captain what I had seen.

Senator SMITH.

What did he say?

Mr. BOXHALL.

He said all right, and then the order came out for the boats.

Senator SMITH.

You mean the order was given to man or lower the lifeboats?

Mr. BOXHALL.

To clear the lifeboats.

Senator SMITH.

Do you know anything about what the carpenter did after you left him?

Mr. BOXHALL.

No, sir; I never saw him any more." [61]

Able seaman, Frederick Clench testified on Day 7 at the American Titanic Disaster Hearing that,

"Senator BOURNE.

Will you kindly explain in your own way what occurred just prior and subsequent to the catastrophe?

Mr. CLENCH.

I was asleep in my bunk when the accident occurred, and I was awakened by the crunching and jarring, as if it was hitting up against something.

Senator BOURNE.

Were you sound asleep?

Mr. CLENCH.

I was sound asleep.

Senator BOURNE.

Are you a heavy sleeper?

Mr. CLENCH.

No, sir; it did not take much to wake me. I am a light sleeper. If anybody touches me, I will jump quick. Of course I put on my trousers and I went on deck on the starboard side of the well deck and I saw a lot of ice.

Senator BOURNE.

On the deck itself?

Mr. CLENCH.

On the deck itself.

Senator BOURNE.

What deck was that?

Mr. CLENCH.

The well deck, sir. With that, I went in the alleyway again under the forecastle head to come down and put on my shoes. Some one said to me, "Did you hear the rush of water?" I said, "No." They said, "Look down under the hatchway." I looked down under the hatchway and I saw the tarpaulin belly out as if there was a lot of wind under it, and I heard the rush of water coming through.

Senator BOURNE.

You heard that?

Mr. CLENCH.

Yes.

Senator BOURNE.

How soon after you struck? How many minutes, would you think?

Mr. CLENCH.

I should say about 10 minutes, sir."[62]

Able bodied Seaman Samuel Hemming testified on day seven of the American Titanic Disaster Hearing that,

"*Senator SMITH.*

Where were you the night of this accident?

Mr. HEMMING.

I was in my bunk.

Senator SMITH.

Were you asleep?

Mr. HEMMING.

Yes, sir.

Senator SMITH.

Were you awakened by anybody?

Mr. HEMMING.

I was awakened by the impact, sir.

Senator SMITH.

What did you do when you were awakened?

Mr. HEMMING.

I went out and put my head through the porthole to see what we hit. I made the remark to the storekeeper {possibly J. Foley}. "It must have been ice." I said, "I do not see anything."

Senator SMITH.

What made you think it was ice?

Mr. HEMMING.

Because I could not see anything.

Senator SMITH.

You mean you looked to see if you saw the lights of another boat, and, not being able to see any such thing, you thought it was ice?

Mr. HEMMING.

Yes, sir.

Senator SMITH.

Had you ever seen ice in that part of the ocean before?

Mr. HEMMING.

No, sir.

Senator SMITH.

Had you ever been through that part before, on your route?

Mr. HEMMING.

Yes, sir.

Senator SMITH.

What did you do then?

Mr. HEMMING.

I went up under the forecastle head to see where the hissing noise came from.

Senator SMITH.

What did you find?

Mr. HEMMING.

Nothing.

Senator SMITH.

Go right along and tell what you did.

Mr. HEMMING.

I did not see anything. I opened the forepeak storeroom; me and the storekeeper went down as far as the top of the tank and found everything dry.

I came up to ascertain where the hissing noise was still coming from. I found it was the air escaping out of the exhaust of the tank.

At that time the chief officer, Mr. Wilde, put his head around the hawse pipe and says: "What is that, Hemming?" I said: "The air is escaping from the forepeak tank. She is making water in the forepeak tank, but the storeroom is quite dry." He said, "All right," and went away.

Senator SMITH.

What did you do then?

Mr. HEMMING.

I went back and turned in.

Senator SMITH.

Do you mean that you went back to your bunk and went to sleep?

Mr. HEMMING.

Me and the storekeeper went back and turned into our bunks.

Senator SMITH.

How long did you stay in your bunks?

Mr. HEMMING.

We went back in our bunks a few minutes. Then the joiner {possibly J. Hutchinson} came in and he said: "If I were you, I would turn out, you fellows. She is making water, one-two-three, and the racket court is getting filled up."

Just as he went, the boatswain came, and he says, "Turn out, you fellows," he says; "you haven't half an hour to live." He said: "That is from Mr. Andrews." He said: "Keep it to yourselves, and let no one know." [63]

The *Titanic* had received a mortal wound when she struck the iceberg. Inside of compartment one was a watertight ballast tank, the forepeak tank which, as stated earlier, did not have a cellular double hull, and the skin of the ship, one inch steel plates, was its only protection against the sea. This tank at the time of the crash had been savagely ripped open and was filling with water. Within ten minutes, fourteen feet of water had the first three holds as well as the Fireman's Passage and Boiler Room #6. Water was also filling Boiler Room #5, but not at the same rate of flooding as the other compartments.

Forty minutes after the collision, their sleeping quarters in the bow in Hold #2 having been flooded with three feet of water, the firemen congregated around the forecastle head.

As able Bodied Seaman Edward J. Buley testified to Senator Fletcher on Day 7 at the American *Titanic* Disaster Hearings:

"EJB066. Do you know when the water began to come into the ship?

- Yes, sir; a little after she struck. You could hear it.

EJB067. Immediately?

- You could hear it immediately. Down where we were, there was a hatchway, right down below, and there was a tarpaulin across it, with an iron batten. You could hear the water rushing in, and the

pressure of air underneath it was such that you could see this bending. In the finish I was told it blew off.

EJB068. What part of the ship would you call that?

- The forecastle head.

EJB069. How far was that from the bow?

- About 20 yards, I should think.

EJB070. That condition could not have obtained unless the steel plates had been torn off from the side of the ship?

- From the bottom of the ship. It was well underneath the water line.

EJB071. And the plates must have been ripped off by the iceberg?

- Yes, sir." [64]

When the *Titanic* hit the iceberg with a speed of approximately 22 knots, with a mass of 52,210 tons, she hit the iceberg with a force of 1,173,200 foot tons. Captain Knapp, during his testimony on day seventeen at the American *Titanic* Disaster Hearings described the collision as follows:

"Senator SMITH.

Have you any means, from the description of the ice to which you have just referred and the speed of the Titanic, which was at that time making about 75 revolutions of her propeller per minute, of knowing the force of the impact?

Capt. KNAPP.

It is impossible, under the testimony as given, to state just how direct a blow the Titanic struck the ice, but an idea may be formed as to the possible blow by using the accepted formula, the weight multiplied by the square of the velocity divided by twice *the gravity. Multiplying the weight of the ship by the square of its speed in feet per second and dividing by twice the force of gravity will give the blow that would have been struck if she had kept straight on her course against this apparently solid mass of ice, which, at a speed of 21 knots, would have been equal to 1,173,200 foot tons, or energy enough to lift 14 monuments the size of the Washington Monument in one second of time. I think from the evidence before your committee it is shown that the ship struck the berg before she had appreciably lost any headway, due either to change of helm or stoppage or reversal of engines, in which event her striking energy would be practically that given above.*

Senator SMITH.

Captain, in view of the strength of this blow, can you account for the apparent absence of shock, the shock seeming to have been scarcely noticeable by the passengers and crew?

Capt. KNAPP.

A comparison might be made to striking a sharp instrument a glancing blow with the hand. There would be no apparent resisting shock. That part of the ice which cut into its outer skin was struck by the ship very much like the edge of a knife would be so struck by the hand. If the ship had struck end on solidly against the mass of ice, then there would have been the shock that takes place when a moving body meets an immovable body."[65]

Over the years, there has been a lot of discussion regarding the quality of the three million rivets that were used to hold the ship together. However, considering the massive force with which the *Titanic* hit the iceberg, it is doubtful that any ship given the times in which it was built, would have survived such a tremendous blow.

Looking back to 1912, it would seem that the *Titanic* was a victim of circumstances. She was the largest passenger ship in the world at that time and she was built using what we would consider today to be outdated engineering concepts, questionable design and was piloted by crews that had very little experience with ships of this size. In other words, the *Titanic* had outgrown the limits of technology of 1912 and was pushing the edge of the envelope. Two concrete examples of the this are two events that occurred with the only two Olympic class ships in existence at the time, the *RMS Olympic* and *RMS Titanic*. These events were identical in nature and were caused by the large displacements of the two ships that in turn created a strong suction that would attract near by ships. In the case of the *Olympic*, the suction pulled the *RMS Hawke* into her side causing a collision and a great deal of damage to both ships. In the case of the *Titanic*, while leaving her berth at Southampton to begin her maiden voyage, her suction ripped the docked ship *SS New York* away from its moorings and almost colliding with it, missing her by a distance of approximately four feet. Oddly enough, Captain Smith was on the Bridge and the Master of both ships.

The mystery that still remains unanswered is why did the *Titanic* sink so fast? In the *Titanic* films, Thomas Andrews, the Titanic's architect tells Captain Smith how long the ship has to survive by taking an inspection tour of the damage and then consulting the ships blueprints. Andrews estimated that the ship had one to one and one half hours to live. [66] Actually, the *Titanic* survived for two hours and forty minutes, much longer than Andrews calculated. This longer survival time was due to the heroic efforts made by the engineers on the ship who probably kept the pumps going for as long as they could.

There is of course, a dramatic element to be added to any of the *Titanic* films by having Andrews be the prophet of doom in a way which allows for the suspense to build by having him set a time line that the ship only had one hour to one and one half hours to live. Therefore, when the Marconi operator Phillips told Captain Smith that the Carpathia was fifty-eight miles away and was coming as fast as she could, Smith and the movie audience knew that the arrival of the Carpathia would be in approximately 4 hours and that the ship was already doomed.

The dichotomy of all of this is that, even though Captain Smith knew he had very little time, lifeboats were still partially filled. Captain Smith's behavior would suggest that he believed that he would have enough time to have the partially filled lifeboats come around to the bow gangways where they could be boarded by additional passengers. In retrospect, it looks very much like Captain Smith may not have believed Andrew's one hour to one and one half hour timeline and was hoping that the *Titanic* would remain afloat until help arrived.

We know that the *Titanic* sank in about two hours and forty minutes, but many questions remain unanswered. Did the ship sink so rapidly because of a narrow crack or ruptured seam that extended along the starboard side of the *Titanic* below the waterline and somehow positioned itself in such a manner to invade the watertight integrity of six watertight compartments? Is it possible that this open seam or crack which would equal the area of a twelve square foot hole could have allowed so much water into the *Titanic* that she sank and broke apart in approximately two and one half hours? Why did Captain Smith delay the process of filling the lifeboats to capacity? Was it possible that Captain Smith disregarded the time line given by Andrews and actually believed that everyone would survive or did something unexpected happen that cost him his life along with that of over fifteen hundred other souls? These questions are what we will now explore.

CHAPTER 7
LEGEND VS. THEORY

One of the curious aspects of the "urban legend" and Hollywood film's vision of this maritime tragedy is that they say absolutely nothing about other possible causes for the rapid sinking of the *Titanic* except making references to the continuous three hundred foot gash or twelve square foot hole theory. But it is equally possible that Able Bodied Seaman Edward J. Buley, as quoted in Chapter 6, hit the nail squarely on the head when he said the bottom was ripped out of the *Titanic* by the iceberg.

David G. Brown in *The Last Log Of The Titanic* advances the theory that the *Titanic* running aground on a submerged shelf of the iceberg. In Mr. Brown's book, we see the *Titanic* missing the surface portion of the iceberg, but slamming at a speed of approximately 22 knots into a submerged ice shelf that literally ripped the bottom out of the ship. Why did the collision seem to be so slight that few passengers were awakened?

The answer may be that when the Titanic sliced its way across the frozen submerged shelf of the iceberg with a force of 1,173,200 foot tons,[67] the bottom was surgically removed by the submerged ice shelf much like a guillotine removing the head of its victim. It has often been said that the victim of the guillotine only feels a slight tingling on the back of the neck when the blade falls. Actually, no one knows how it feels since no one has ever returned from the other side to tell us, but fortunately, we have countless descriptions of the collision from 705 survivors of the *Titanic* disaster. A few of the words used to describe the collision were that the collision was like a "shuddering", a "quivering", a dull "thump", a "bum" and a "grating" noise. It is clear that the collision was not was like a head on crash between two steam locomotives; however, there is strong evidence to support the fact that the passenger's opinion as to the severity of the collision was largely due to the passenger's location on the ship at the moment of impact.

The Titanic was 882 feet, nine inches long and that is the equivalent of over three north and south New York City blocks, a distance of 264 feet per city block. The sleeping quarters for the Third Class passengers was in the bow and stern section of the ship. Unfortunately, only three of Third Class survivors testified during the inquiry at the US Senate Inquiry and none testified at the British Wreck Commissioner's Inquiry. Therefore, the bulk of the descriptions regarding the impact were made by First and Second Class passengers as well as crew members. The First and Second Class passengers quarters were in the middle third of the ship and were therefore a city block away from the point of impact. A Third Class passenger reported to a local newspaper that she was thrown from her bunk at the moment of impact and one member of the crew who's sleeping quarters was in the bow, testified that he was awakened by a grating sound and thought the ship was dropping anchor. In contrast, First Class passengers Edith Russell, referred to the collision as a "bump".

It would seem that the speed of the *Titanic*, combined with her mass of 52,310 tons, produced a deadly collision force of 1,173,200 foot tons that, in a matter of ten seconds, crushed her bow and ripped out her bottom. It must be remembered that despite the hype accompanying her construction, the *Titanic* was no super ship. She was built using the technology of 1912 and used over three million rivets to hold the steel plates together thus forming a barrier to the sea. If the description of the location of the collision point on the *Titanic's* starboard bow was accurately described by Fleet and others, it would seem logical that the ship, having an upward curved bow would have run aground on the submerged ice shelf. As Murdoch attempted his "port around" the iceberg, he exacerbated the situation and the ice shelf acted much like a pathologist microtome blade, slicing off the starboard bow section of the bottom while cutting through the fireman's tunnel. If you look carefully at any blueprint of the *Titanic*, you will notice the upward turned bow bottom of the ship. As this curved bottom approached the underwater ledge, the ice sliced open the Peak Tank, Holds #1, #2, #3 and also had direct access to the Fireman's Passage and possibly Boiler Room #6. As the rivets popped and the steel plates fell to the ocean floor, the sea began to invade the bowels of the Titanic at a rapid rate.

PROPOSED ICE DAMAGE

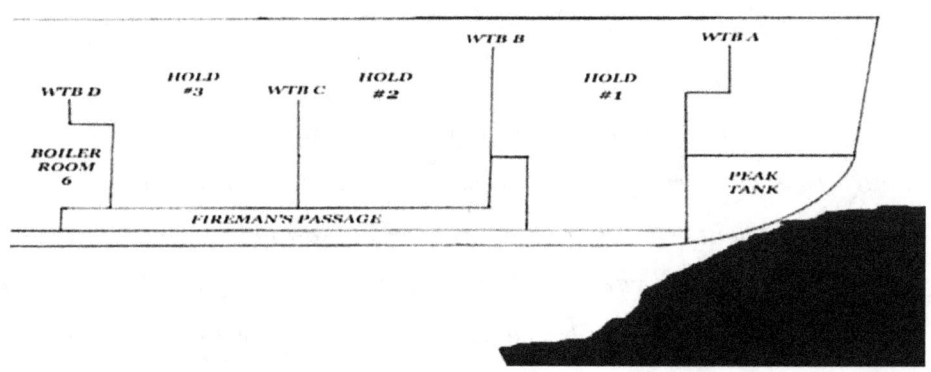

FIGURE 6

The "Port Around" maneuver, of course, was not the only problem. As mentioned before, the port and starboard extremities of the bow, lacking as they did a double bottom, provided the *Titanic* with an Achilles Heel since this led directly to the first four "watertight" compartments being directly exposed to the sea. Therefore, the *Titanic* hit the iceberg at the starboard bow, its Achilles Heel. Boiler Rooms #6 and #5 had their hull plates ruptured as described by Frederick Barrett by the shifting of the center of gravity of the iceberg as the *Titanic* ran onto the underwater ledge and holing the starboard turn of the bilge as described by David G. Brown. [68] A final point to consider would be the damage that would have been caused by the interconnected structures. Given this factor, it would be easy to conclude that all of these lead to the rapid flooding and breaking apart of the *Titanic* in just two hours and forty minutes.

Unfortunately, the *Titanic* crashed into the ocean floor and buried herself into sixty feet of mud. We may never be able to examine its bow or bottom, but we do have testimony of the survivors that support David G. Brown's theory, including that of Mr. Hugh Woolner on day ten of the US Senate Inquiry.

"*Senator SMITH.*
When did you first know of the impact?
Mr. WOOLNER.
We felt it under the smoking room. We felt a sort of stopping, a sort of, not exactly shock, but a sort of slowing down; and then we sort of felt a rip that gave a sort of a slight twist to the whole room. Everybody, so far as I could see, stood up and a number of men walked out rapidly through the swinging doors on the port side, and ran along to the rail that was behind the mast - I think there was a mast standing out there - and the rail just beyond." [69]

And there is Quartermaster Hitchens testifying on day five of the American Disaster Hearings,

"*Senator SMITH.*
Who gave the first order?
Mr. HICHENS.
Mr. Murdoch, the first officer, sir; the officer in charge. The sixth officer repeated the order, "The helm is hard astarboard, sir." But, during the time, she was crushing the ice, or we could hear the grinding noise along the ship's bottom. I heard

the telegraph ring, sir. The skipper came rushing out of his room - Capt. Smith - and asked, "What is that?" Mr. Murdoch said, "An iceberg." He said, "Close the emergency doors."[70]

Also Third Officer, Herbert J. Pitman testified on day four at the US Senate Inquiry in Washington,

"Senator SMITH.

Was there any special impact to awaken you?

Mr. PITMAN.

No; there was a sound that I thought seemed like the ship coming to an anchor - the chain running out over the windlass.

Senator SMITH.

Did this impact jar the ship?

Mr. PITMAN.

No; it gave just a little vibration. I was about half awake and about half asleep. It did not quite awaken me.

Senator SMITH.

Did you arouse yourself?

Mr. PITMAN.

I did, after a little thinking, wondering where we were anchoring." [71]

Steerage passenger Daniel Buckley, one of only three steerage passengers that were called to testify at the American Titanic Disaster Hearings on day thirteen relived the moment of impact,

"Senator SMITH.

Did you feel a shock from the collision when the ship struck?

Mr. BUCKLEY.

Yes; I did.

Senator SMITH.

And did that wake you up?

Mr. BUCKLEY.

It did. I did not feel any shock in the steamer; only just heard a noise. I heard a kind of a grating noise.

Senator SMITH.

Did you get right out of bed?

Mr. BUCKLEY.

Yes; I did.

Senator SMITH.

When you got out, you got into the water? There was water in your compartment in the steerage?

Mr. BUCKLEY.

Yes; water was there slightly. There was not very much.

Senator SMITH.

How much?

Mr. BUCKLEY.

The floor was only just getting wet. It was only coming in under the door very slightly."[72]

Mr. Rowlett, leading Fireman on the Titanic also testified at the British Wreck Commission Hearings,

"4854. You were going to turn in?

- I was going to turn in and the same man, Ford, came back and said there was water coming in down below, that is down the spiral staircase.

4855. Did you look down the staircase?

- Yes.

4856. Did you see the water?

- I saw the water rushing in.

4857. Just let us have it clear where that is. Do you see this plan?

- Yes.

4858. Is that it (Pointing on the plan.)?

- The lowest of all.

4859. *You looked down here and saw it?*

- Yes, I saw the water rushing in here. (Pointing on the plan.) I saw it running out of the fore part of the pipe tunnel right down at the bottom of the stairs.

Mr. Rowlatt:

That is what it is marked upon the map, my Lord - "pipe tunnel."

The Witness:

That is the tunnel we go through from our quarters to go into the stokehold.

The Attorney-General:

"Firemens Passage and Pipe Tunnel." You will find it on the same plan as the tank top we were looking at before.

The Commissioner:

He got into the firemen's passage I understand?

Mr. Rowlatt:

No, he did not, my Lord.

4860. *(To the Witness.) You looked down the staircase?*

- Yes, the staircase leading to the stokehold.

Mr. Rowlatt:

Your Lordship sees the spiral there.

4861. *(The Commissioner.) Where were you looking?*

- Down the spiral stairway.

4862. *And where did it lead from and to?*

- From our quarter to the stokehold, No. 11 stokehold, No. 6 section.

4863. *(Mr. Rowlatt.) The spiral staircase led down to the bottom of the ship, and from there the fireman's passage and pipe tunnel led along to No. 6 section?*

- No. 6 section, No. 11 stokehold.

4864. *Now where you saw the water coming - you saw it coming from aft, forward into the bottom of the spiral staircase?*

- From the starboard side.

4865. *Are there two staircases?*

- *Only one. There are two staircases, one up and one down, but there is only one our side. I was looking down the one on the port side - not down the staircase, but at the side of the staircase.*

4866. *You were looking down on the port side of the staircase?*

- *Yes, and saw the water rushing in from the starboard side at the bottom.*

4867. *Are there two spiral staircases in that part of the ship or one?*

- *Two. They are marked distinctly, one for going down and one for coming up.*

4868. *Which of the two were you looking down?*

- *I was looking down the port one.*

4869. *Now is there a communication between the bottom of that spiral staircase and the bottom of the other one?*

- *It is all open, just a handrail to go along.*

4870. *The water which you saw rushing down there could not have come from forward, could it, because there is a bulkhead across?*

- *It came from the ship's side I am telling you, the starboard side.*

4871. *You could not see where it was coming in, but you saw it coming from the starboard side?*

- *I saw it coming from the ship's side.*

4872. *When you want to go aft along the passage, how long is it before you come to a watertight door?*

- *At the bottom of the tunnel.*

4873. *How far on - how far had you to go before you got to the first stokehold that you come to?*

- *I could not give you the distance. There are two watertight doors there, I know.*

4874. *There are two bulkheads?*

- *Yes, about 6 feet apart. There is one here, and the other is about 6 feet away from it.*

4875. *It is marked there "coffer-dam watertight" - do you know what that means?*

- *No.*

4876. *When you get down to the bottom of this staircase this tunnel runs amidships straight aft?*

- *Yes, straight aft.*

4877. *Amidships?*

- *Yes.*

4878. *Then do you go some little way before you come to the first watertight door?*

- *Yes.*

4879. *Then you go through that and you go about the same distance before you come to the next one?*

- *No, they are about 6 feet apart, those two watertight doors.*

4880. *Are those two watertight doors both close up against the stokehold?*

- *Yes.*

4881. *Till you get there you do not have a watertight door before?*

- *No, we get down through the tunnel leading to the stokehold.*

Mr. Rowlatt:

It is very obscure upon the plan, my Lord.

(*The Solicitor-General explains the plan to the Commissioner.*)

4882. (*The Commissioner.*) *Now, Mr. Rowlatt, in order that we may have it on the Note, I want you to state the effect of this Witness's evidence; let him listen to you and say whether it is right. (To the Witness.) Have you heard what I said?*

- *Yes, Sir.*

The Commissioner:

Now, listen to this gentleman and see whether he tells us what you have been saying, and tells it properly.

4883. (*Mr. Rowlatt.*) *There are two spiral staircases which go down to the bottom of the ship, one for going down and the other for coming up?*

- *Yes.*

4884. And they go down in the same space?

- Yes.

4885. And when they get to the bottom they both reach a fireman's passage, which is like a tunnel running amidships fore and aft?

- Yes.

4886. And you go along that from the bottom of the spiral staircase aft until you come just before where you get into the foremost stokehold, No. 6 boiler section, and at that point you go through two watertight doors in a space of about 6 feet. Is that right?

- Yes, before you reach the stokehold.

4887. And as you are going down that tunnel on your right hand and on your left there will be iron bulkheads?

- Yes.

4888. Whether those are watertight or not, I suppose you do not know?

- They are iron bulkheads, one on each side.

4889. (The Commissioner.) Are they watertight or not?

- I could not tell you that; I do not know.

Mr. Laing:

Yes, they are.

The Commissioner:

But this Witness does not know it.

4890. (Mr. Rowlatt.) No, my Lord. (To the Witness.) But what I want to get from you is this. You said you saw the water coming from the ship's side; do you mean that. You saw it coming through the ship's side?

- No, coming from the ship's side.

4891. That was merely the direction from which you saw it travelling?

- Yes.

4892. That is, into the space into which the spiral staircase is descending?

- Yes.

4893. *You could not tell whether the water was coming through the fore and aft bulkhead at the bottom of the staircase, could you?*

- No, I could only see the direction it came from.

4894. *Was it coming hard?*

- Yes, it was more than rushing in; it was falling in.

4895. *Did it strike you it was coming in at a point which was not at the bottom of the bulkhead?*

- Well, you could not exactly tell that. There was a lot of water there and from the way it was rushing in you could not exactly tell how it was coming." [73]

During the British Wreck Inquiry questioning of Mr. Edward Wilding, Naval Architect and employee of Harland and Wolfe on day nineteen, there was a lengthy discussion about the water that entered the Fireman's Passage immediately after the collision with the iceberg during which, he suggested, that there was a possibility that a chunk of ice could have punctured the ship's hull above the turn of the bilge, extending 3.3 feet between Mr. Wilding and Mr. Clement Edwards who was questioning Mr. Wilding. It was during this discussion that there seemed to be a bit of incredulity expressed by Mr. Edwards as to the possibility of a chunk of ice that would have punctured the hull of the Titanic above the turn of the bilge and somehow extended 3.3 feet into the ship and puncture the starboard side of the watertight Fireman's Passage at the spiral staircase. Note his response to the following question:

"20714. *And you said that as that inner skin was a certain distance - I think you said at 3 feet 6 inches?*

- 3 feet 3 inches, I think it is.

20715. *That as the water was coming through there it is quite clear the ice must have penetrated at least that distance?*

- I agreed to a suggestion of that sort.

20716. *I am glad you call it a suggestion, because I am not aware of any definite evidence here that water was coming in through that skin on the side of the spiral staircase?*

- Look at Hendrickson's evidence, and you will see it. He saw water rushing from the starboard side at the bottom of the spiral stair.

20717. *He said he could not tell where it was coming from, it was such a rush?*

- But he saw it coming from the starboard side.

20718. *That is the starboard side?*

- At the foot of the spiral stair.

20719. *It would be possible for water to be coming from the starboard side to have either been coming out fore of the spiral staircase or a little aft. That is to say, even supposing water was coming more or less from that side, that is not in itself conclusive that there was penetration in the area of the spiral staircase?*

- The spiral staircase being in a watertight trunk both at the fore end and across the fore end, and at the side and at the afterend, some part of it must have been penetrated. I mean the side and end and bottom are all watertight, and water can only get in if there is some penetration.

20720. *I agree, but whether that penetration is off the spiral staircase on the starboard side or is actually on the starboard side or is even fore of the spiral staircase -?*

- But let me point out the spiral staircase occupies practically the whole dimension of that trunk, consequently there must be penetration of the trunk which immediately surrounds the spiral stair.

20721. *Does that follow?*

- How could water get through the watertight space if you do not make a hole in it?

20722. *Allow me for a moment. Is it not possible that water might have come in through the floor of the ship?*

- Through the floor of the spiral stair, not of the ship.

20723. *Hendrickson's evidence, I think, is rather important. Hendrickson said, in reply to question 4859: "You looked down here and saw it? - (A.) Yes, I saw the water rushing in here. (Pointing on the plan.) I saw it running out of the forepart of the pipe tunnel right down at the bottom of the stairs"?*

- Now it is not quite clear, but, of course, it is reasonable that he should call the trunk which surrounds the spiral stair part of the pipe tunnel, and it is in practice. I am only putting to you what I think is the probable explanation." [74]

From the testimony given above, it is clear that the *Titanic* ran aground on a submerged shelf of an iceberg on the evening of April 14, 1912, the ship's bow sliding up onto the ice shelf as Murdoch was attempting a "port around". With Murdoch's eyes fixed firmly on the part of the iceberg he could see above the sea, he was unfortunately oblivious to what was below the bow of the *Titanic*. The rest, as they say, is history.

As described by Mr. Brown, the *Titanic* ran aground on the ice shelf and then pivoted around the iceberg, thus changing its course from a westerly direction almost due north. As she struck the ice shelf, Fleet testified during the United States Senate Inquiry on day five that the *Titanic* listed to port,

Senator FLETCHER.

Did it strike the bow or just back of the bow?

Mr. FLEET.

Just about in front of the foremast.

Senator FLETCHER.

Did it tilt the ship to any extent?

Mr. FLEET.

She listed to port right afterwards.

Senator FLETCHER.

To what extent?

Mr. FLEET.

I could not say; a slight list.

Senator FLETCHER.

Just immediately on striking the berg?

Mr. FLEET.

Just afterwards.

Senator FLETCHER.

Did it seem that the blow came beneath the surface of the water and caused her to shift?

Mr. FLEET.

Yes, sir." [75]

This listing testimony almost certainly proves that the *Titanic* ran aground on a submerged ice shelf, shifting the center of gravity of the iceberg, making the surface portion of the iceberg, tip toward the *Titanic* and bump against the starboard side of the ship and according to Fourth Officer Boxhall, depositing ice on the starboard side of the Forecastle Well Deck and A deck as described earlier by Ms. Edith Russell, First Class passenger.

In a matter of ten seconds, the starboard bow bottom of the *Titanic* was damaged starting at the Forepeak and extending through Holds #1, #2 and #3, as the iceberg ripped apart the starboard non-double hull bilge section as well as the double hulled starboard side of the Fireman's Passage from Hold #1 and #2. As the ship continued to slide across the ice shelf, she damaged her bilge on the starboard side of the Titanic in Boiler Room #6 and #5 as described by Frederick Barrett. The combined damage led to the immediate flooding of the Forepeak, Hold #1, Hold #2, Hold #3, and Boiler Room #6 and #5.

In the end, the *Titanic* sustained massive structural damage to her starboard bow, her bottom and her starboard hull below the waterline. It is doubtful that Captain Smith or anyone else, for that matter, could have immediately grasped the severity of the damage. In this moment of confusion and incomplete damage reports from 4th Officer Boxhall, the captain started up her engines for the final time, in a desperate attempt to reach Halifax. But once aware of the damage that had been done to the bow and turn of the bilge, Captain Smith finally realized that it was too late to save his ship and issued the orders to stop the engines for the final time and to uncover the lifeboats.

With his ship sinking beneath his feet, the ship's orchestra playing in the background and distress rockets being fired into the inky blackness of the star studded sky, Captain Smith raised the curtain on the final act of the *Titanic* tragedy by ordering women and children to be loaded into the lifeboats. As he watched the human drama begin to unfold, knowing full well that there were not enough lifeboats for everyone on board and that the *Carpathia* would not arrive in time to rescue for those unfortunate souls that remained behind, himself included, he must have been forced to accept the fact that his ship would soon be bound for eternity.

CHAPTER 8
EXPLOSIONS

According to the *Titanic* "urban legend", there were no explosions on board the ship as it sank. Instead, after the ship hit the iceberg, it filled up with water, went down by the head and in the 1997 film *Titanic*, broke in half and went straight to the bottom without any boiler explosions. With the exception of the Hollywood 1953 film *Titanic* that shows boiler explosions as the ship floundered, Hollywood and others seemingly ignore the testimony made by the survivors who testified that there were explosions minutes before the *Titanic* made its final plunge as described by Archie Jewell, Lookout on the Titanic, British Wreck Commissioner's Inquiry British Wreck Commission, day two:

"175. Just tell us shortly what you yourself saw then. What did you see that happened to the "Titanic" before she went down and as she went down?

- We stopped there and watched her gradually sink away. We could see the people about on the deck before the lights went out. As she went away by the head so the lights went out, and we heard some explosions as she was going down. But all the lights went out and we could only see a black object in front of us."[76]

Mrs. J. Stuart White, First Class passenger testified on Day 11 at the American Titanic Disaster Hearings that,

"Senator SMITH.

What was your impression of it as it went down?

Mrs. WHITE.

It was something dreadful.

Nobody ever thought the ship was going down. I do not think there was a person that night, I do not think there was a man on the boat who thought the ship was going down. They speak of the bravery of the men. I do not think there was any particular bravery, because none of the men thought it was going down. If they had thought the ship was going down, they would not have frivoled as they did about it. Some of them said, "When you come back you will need a pass," and, "You can not get on tomorrow morning without a pass." They never would have said these things if anybody had had any idea that the ship was going to sink.

In my opinion the ship when it went down was broken in two. I think very probably it broke in two.

I heard four distinct explosions, which we supposed were the boilers. Of course, we did not know anything about it.

Senator SMITH.

How loud were those explosions?

Mrs. WHITE.

They were tremendous." [77]

In the book, *Wreck and Sinking of the Titanic*, Edited by Marshall Everett, 1912, page 82, Mr. John Snyder and his wife said,

"We went about 200 yards from the Titanic. We could see nothing wrong except that the big boat seemed to be settling at the bow. Still we could not make ourselves believe that the Titanic would sink. But the Titanic continued to settle and we could see the passengers plunging about the decks and heard their cries.

"We moved fatrher away. Suddenly there came two sharp explosions as the water rushed into the boilers room and the boilers exploded. The explosions counteracted the effect of the suction made when the big boat went to the bottom and it is more than probable that this saved some of the lifeboats from being drawn to the bottom." [78]

On the eleventh day of the United States Senate Inquiry, Archibald Gracie testified in response to Senator Smith's questions about his experiences abandoning the ship:

"Senator SMITH.

So far as you know, was this boat to which you have referred put to any use that night?

Mr. GRACIE.

Yes.

Senator SMITH.

Describe it.

Mr. GRACIE.

That is the boat that I came to when I came up from below. I was taken down with the ship, and hanging on to that railing, but I soon let go. I felt myself whirled around, swam under water, fearful that the hot water that came up from the boilers might boil me up - and the second officer (Editors Note, Officer Lightoller) told me that he had the same feeling - swam it seemed to me with unusual strength, and succeeded finally in reaching the surface and in getting a good distance away from the ship." [79]

Oddly enough, there is conflicting testimony given by Lightoller himself who said that there were no boiler explosions and yet also testified that as the ship sank, he was pinned against a wire grating that covered an airshaft that delivered fresh air to the lower decks. As the ship sank, water poured into the shaft and the current pinned Lightoller against the wire grating. Lightoller then described a blast of hot air that carried him to the surface. This could only be the result of a boiler explosion. Lightoller's exact testimony is as follows:

"United States Senate Inquiry, Day 1, Testimony of Charles H. Lightoller
Senator SMITH.

What would be the effect of water at about freezing on the boilers?

Mr. LIGHTOLLER.

It is an open question. I have heard it said that they will explode, and others say they will not.

Senator SMITH.

Have you ever known of a case?

Mr. LIGHTOLLER.

Of a case in point?

Senator SMITH.

Where they have exploded?

Mr. LIGHTOLLER.

I was sucked down, and I was blown out with something pretty powerful when the ship went down.

Senator SMITH.

After the ship went down?

Mr. LIGHTOLLER.

Yes.

Senator SMITH.

Just describe that a little more fully. You were sucked down?

Mr. LIGHTOLLER.

I was sucked against the blower first of all. As I say, I was on top of the officers' quarters, and there was nothing more to be done. The ship then took a dive, and I turned face forward and also took a dive.

Senator SMITH.

From which side?

Mr. LIGHTOLLER.

From on top, practically amidships; a little to the starboard side, where I had got to; and I was driven back against a blower - which is a large thing that shape (indicating) which faces forward to the wind and which then goes down to the stokehole. But there is a grating there, and it was against this grating that I was sucked by the water and held there.

Senator SMITH.

Was your head above water?

Mr. LIGHTOLLER.

No, sir.

Senator SMITH.

You were under water?

Mr. LIGHTOLLER.

Yes, sir. And then this explosion, or whatever it was, took place. Certainly, I think it was the boilers exploded. There was a terrific blast of air and water, and I was blown out clear.

Senator SMITH.

Was there any debris that was blown above the surface?

Mr. LIGHTOLLER.

That I could not say." [80]

You have read in Chapter 4 a description of how the electricity that powered the *Titanic's* electric lights was generated to the effect that the ship had four main dynamos powered by steam that was generated from Boiler Rooms #1, #2 and #4. You will remember that the boiler rooms were numbered backwards starting with Boiler Room #6 located beneath the first funnel near the bow, and Boiler Room #1 which was located below the third funnel of the ship, near the stern.

Two emergency dynamos on D deck powered the lights in all passenger and machinery areas, passageways, stairways and the Boat Deck all receiving their primary steam supply from Boiler Rooms, #2, #3 and #5. In addition, there was a connecting steam line that could connect the emergency dynamos to any of the six boiler rooms if needed.

After the *Titanic* hit the iceberg, it was clear that there was no direct ice damage to the ship abaft Boiler Room #5. It is also known that the watertight doors abaft of the main engine room were opened to allow the ship's Engineers to move freely back and forth as they tried in vain to stem the tide of rising water. It would be logical to conclude, therefore, that the firemen could and did maintain a head of steam in some of the boilers in order to keep the lights burning throughout the ship so they could see what they were doing and also to power the pumps that were fighting a loosing battle with the rising water. Unfortunately, we will never have their testimony since none of the Engineers survived the sinking.

From the description given by the survivors however, we do know that the lights remained on right up to the final moments, powered by, necessity, the emergency and the main electric dynamos. In all probability, Boiler Room #2 was the source of this power since it was not damaged by the iceberg, was the furthest away from the damaged hull in Boiler Room #5, and Boiler Room #1 was not in use since there was no coal in the bunkers because of the coal strike.

It is evident from the eyewitness reports that the lights remained on to the last and then, just before the ship disappeared beneath the waves, suddenly went dark, as if someone had pulled the plug on a Christmas tree as the *Titanic* vanished into the darkness of the cold Atlantic. It is this sudden loss of power and explosions that make one assume that the Boiler Room #2 was being used to power the main dynamos and the emergency dynamos on D deck. When the ship went dark, it also immediately broke apart in a series of explosions that the survivors vividly described.

The area that the ship broke apart was immediately beneath the third funnel that provided the exhaust for the Boiler Rooms #1 and #2. When the ship broke apart, the watertight compartments in Boiler Room #2 flooded, the boilers exploded and the dynamos stopped producing electricity since they no longer had sufficient steam to carry on. It is interesting to note that in 1985 when Dr. Ballard first discovered the remains of the *Titanic*, one of his first images on the television monitor was that of a boiler resting on the ocean floor. It was later determined that this boiler came from Boiler room #1.

In the year 2000, David Concannon, who was participating in an expedition to collect artifacts from the *Titanic* observed pieces of the ships bottom resting on the ocean floor. Because of technical difficulties, he did not photograph them and, therefore, could not document his findings. Five years later, he contacted John Chatterton and Richie Kohler. In the book, *TITANIC'S LAST SECRETS,* written by Brad Matsen, he describes the discovery and subsequent photographing of these bottom sections, which, it was subsequently determined after extensive investigation, came from the section of the ship immediately below the third funnel, an area that included a section of the tank top and bottom of Boiler Room #1.

Putting these two events together, it is obvious that the *Titanic's* tank top broke apart in and around Boiler Room #1, caused by the bending of the ship, hogging, which resulted in a catastrophic failure of the tank top in Boiler Room #2 and #1 and by the boiler explosions in Boiler Room #2.

George Carvell, coal trimmer, reported during day five of the British Wreck Commission that water was observed coming from the floor of Boiler Room #4,

"4261. *As far as you saw in No. 4, did any water come in from the side of the ship?*

- Not so far as I saw.

4262. *When the water came up through the plates what was done then?*

- We stopped as long as we could.

4263. *That is right?*

- And then I thought to myself it was time I went for the escape ladder.

4264. *They were still drawing the fires, these men, were they?*

- Yes.

4265. *How high did the water get above the plates they were standing on? How much water were they standing in before they left?*

- About a foot." [81]

It was also reported by Thomas P. Dillon, coal trimmer on Day 5 of the British Wreck Commission that,

"3816. Did you see any water before you went up in any of the boiler rooms or the engine room?

- Yes, there was water coming in forward.

3817. The furthest point forward you reached was No. 4 boiler section?

- Yes.

3818. Was it coming in there?

- Yes.

3819. Where was it coming in?

- Coming from underneath.

3820. From underneath the floor?

- Yes." [82]

These observations support the theory presented by many observers that the tank top was bent by the stress of the ship sinking by the head and the stern rising into the air. Initially, there was no damage done to Boiler Room #4. However, one hour and forty minutes later, at approximately twenty past one in the morning, one hour before the *Titanic* sank, water started entering Boiler Room #4 from the tank top. As the ship continued to sink, the rivets in the tank top began to pop, with the result that the steel plates began to loosen and began leaking. Eventually, as the bending continued to apply more stress on the bottom and tank top, the entire tank top began to fail and the boilers that were providing stem for the electric dynamos in Boiler Room #2 exploded, the crew not having had enough time to draw the fires and vent the steam. These explosions further weakened the bottom of the ship from bilge keel to bilge keel beneath the boilers in Boiler Room #1 and along with the "hogging" of the ship, help send approximately five thousand seven hundred and forty square feet of the *Titanic's* bottom to the ocean floor below.

Immediately after the tank top failed, the stern of the ship, which had previously been lifted out of the water now, without the connecting tank top, began to suffer increased structural stress in and around the sidewalls of the hull directly beneath the third funnel which resulted in the hull cracking even more rapidly until the ship finally broke completely in two. The tearing apart of the sidewalls and inner decks created the rumbling sound that other survivors said that they heard as the *Titanic* sank.

As the ship split in two, the contents of the *Titanic* began to spew out of the ship thus creating what it now called the debris field. The bow section being completely separated from the stern sank first. As the survivors watched the stern section reach a vertical position, possibly because of the weight of the reciprocating engines being at the end of the stern section fracture, they were unaware that the ship had already broken apart and that the bow was already on its way to the bottom. Seeing the stern in a vertical position as it disappeared beneath the waves, they believed that the entire ship was still intact. Minutes later however, the bow and aft sections of the *Titanic* reached their final resting place, 12,460 feet beneath the surface of the sea.

CHAPTER 9
300 FOOT GASH VS. GROUNDING THEORY

As described earlier in Chapter 3, out of all of these "urban legends" that have persisted for almost one hundred years, is the belief that the *Titanic* hit an iceberg with a glancing blow and as it glanced off of the burg, it somehow ripped a 300 foot gash in the ship's hull right above the curve of the bilge from the bow, up to and including, Boiler Room #5.

However, this theory was modified in 1985 after Dr. Robert Ballard found the *Titanic* and forever changed after researchers, using a ultrasound technique to examine the starboard side of the hull that was buried sixty feet in the mud, reported six non-continuous gashes instead of one continuous gash, all of them strategically located along the starboard side of the ship, in a position which indicated that the first five watertight compartments had been flooded.

The recent modified version of the six non-continuous gashes does fall in line with Edith Russell's previously given verbal description of the iceberg bumping along the side of the ship. Ms. Russell's statements, combined with the fact that the *Titanic* hit with a force of 1,173,200 foot tons is serious food for thought.

However, as discussed in Chapter 5, researchers, in the process of exploring other theories as to what may have happened that faithful night, have recently started to seriously question the three hundred foot long rip, non-continuous gash and glancing blow legend by suggesting that the *Titanic* could have possibly "grounded" herself on an underwater ice ledge, a "grounding" that led to the bow bottom section of the *Titanic* being ripped asunder, resulting in the first five watertight compartments being flooded at a fantastic rate of speed, as reported in the British Wreck Commission.

"Description of the Damage to the Ship and its Gradual Final Effect
Gradual Effect of the Damage

It will thus be seen that all the six compartments forward of No. 4 boiler room were open to the sea by damage which existed at about 10 feet above the keel. At 10 minutes after the collision the water seems to have risen to about 14 feet above the keel in all these compartments except No. 5 boiler room. After the first ten minutes, the water rose steadily in all these six compartments. The forepeak above the peak tank was not filled until an hour after the collision when the vessel's bow was submerged to above C deck. The water then flowed in from the top through the deck scuttle forward of the collision bulkhead. It was by this scuttle that access was obtained to all the decks below C down to the peak tank top on the Orlop deck.

At 12 o'clock water was coming up in No. 1 hatch. (Lee, 2455, 79) It was getting into the firemen's quarters and driving the firemen out. (2485) It was rushing round No. 1 hatch on G deck and coming mostly from the starboard side, so that in 20 minutes the water had risen above G deck in No. 1 hold. (Pitman, 14962, 65)

In No. 2 hold about 40 minutes after the collision the water was coming in to the seamen's quarters on E deck through a burst fore and aft wooden bulkhead of a third class cabin opposite the seamen's wash place. (Poingdestre, 2844-45) Thus, the water had risen in No. 2 hold to about 3 ft. above E deck in 40 minutes.

In No. 3 hold the mail room was afloat about 20 minutes after the collision. The bottom of the mail room which is on the Orlop deck, is 24 feet above the keel. (Pitman, 14948-49)

The watertight doors on F deck at the fore and after ends of No. 3 compartment were not closed then. (Boxhall, 15757)

The mail room was filling and water was within 2 ft. of G deck, rising fast, when the order was given to clear the boats. (15374, 80) (Johnson, 3397)

There was then no water on F deck.

There is a stairway on the port side on G deck which leads down to the first class baggage room on the Orlop deck immediately below. There was water in this baggage room 25 minutes after the collision. Half an hour after the collision water was up to G deck in the mail room.

Thus the water had risen in this compartment to within 2 ft. of G deck in 20 minutes, and above G deck in 25 to 30 minutes.

No. 6 boiler room was abandoned by the men almost immediately after the collision. Ten minutes later the water had risen to 8 ft. above the top of the double bottom, and probably reached the top of the bulkhead at the after end of the compartment, at the level of E deck, in about one hour after the collision.

In No. 5 boiler room there was no water above the stokehold plates, until a rush of water came through the pass between the boilers from the forward end, and drove the leading stoker out. (Barrett, 1969)

It has already been shown in the description of what happened in the first ten minutes, that water was coming into No. 5 boiler room in the forward starboard bunker at 2 ft. above the plates in a stream about the size of a deck hose. The door in this bunker had been dropped probably when water was first discovered, which was a few minutes after the collision. This would cause the water to be retained in the bunker until it rose high enough to burst the door which was weaker than the bunker bulkhead. This happened about an hour after the collision. (2038, 39, 41)

No. 4 boiler room. *- One hour and 40 minutes after collision water was coming in forward, in No. 4 boiler room, from underneath the floor in the forward part, in small quantities. The men remained in that stokehold till ordered on deck.*

Nos. 3, 2 and 1 boiler rooms. - *When the men left No. 4 some of them went through Nos. 3, 2 and 1 boiler rooms into the reciprocating engine room, and from there on deck. (Dillon, 3795) There was no water in the boiler rooms abaft No. 4 one hour 40 minutes after the collision (1.20 a.m.), (3811) and there was then none in the reciprocating and turbine engine rooms."* [83]

The British Wreck Commission went on to say that,

"It has been shown that water came into the five forward compartments to a height of about 14 feet above the keel in the first ten minutes. This was at a rate of inflow with which the ship's pumps could not possibly have coped, so that the damage done to these five compartments alone inevitably sealed the doom of the ship." [84]

It is extremely difficult to imagine that six independent gashes would collectively have produced a hole of only twelve square feet, at the right location along the starboard side of sufficient size to allow for such massive amounts of water to enter the *Titanic* in such an unbelievable short period of time, particularly when a total area of twelve square feet is the magic number needed to allow a sufficient volume of water into the *Titanic* to sink in the allotted time. But did it really happen?

We know that the twelve square foot hole theory is a reversed engineered number calculated by Edward Wilding, a Harland and Wolff engineer and given as evidence at the British Wreck Commissioner's Inquiry. This number was calculated using the testimony from the survivors as to the levels of water in the ship and the time it took for the water to get to that depth. Using this procedure, Wilding calculated that it would take a crack with a combined total of twelve square feet to sink the ship. It is interesting to note that the six cracks that were discovered do not add up to the magical twelve square foot requirement as pointed out by David G. Brown. According to Mr. Wilding, the twelve square foot hole would equal a crack of three quarters of an inch wide by two hundred feet long. To quote David Brown in his book, *The Last Log of the Titanic*, " If we assume the plates were pushed apart to a uniform one inch, it would have taken 114 linear feet of open seam to equal a 12-square foot hole. Sonic images seems to indicate six open seams totaling 31 meters, or 107.7 feet." [85]

First, consider the fact, as outlined in Chapter 3 that the *Titanic* did not have a double hull on either the starboard or port side of the bow. One inch steel plates alone were the only protection against flooding at this point and unfortunately, it was here that the *Titanic* struck the iceberg with a force of 1,173,200 foot tons. The single bottomed section of the ships starboard bow, including the wall of the peak tank, did not have a ghost of a chance of surviving the stress of the collision. The reason that the passengers and crew were unaware of the massive damage that had occurred is simply that the iceberg's mass was far greater than that of the *Titanic* itself. As the ship struck the underwater ledge of the iceberg traveling as it was, at a speed of approximately 22 knots and did so with a force of 1,173,200 foot tons, the bow and keel section crumpled like the Styrofoam® cup in the hand of Richard Dreyfuss in the film *Jaws*. David G. Brown's book, *The Last Log of the Titanic* explains, how the underwater ledge of the iceberg could have removed the *Titanic*'s keel.

A second point to consider is the Fireman's Passage location, in the center of the ship on the Tank Top Deck, that was flooded five minutes after the collision with the iceberg. It is significant that this area was directly above a double hulled section that started in Hold #2 and extending into Boiler Room #6. According to the British Wreck Commission,

"In No. 2 hold five minutes after the collision water was seen rushing in at the bottom of the firemen's passage on the starboard side, (Hendrickson, 4859) so that the ship's side was damaged abaft of bulkhead B sufficiently to open the side of the firemen's passage, which was 3 1/2 ft. from the outer skin of the ship, thereby flooding both the hold and the passage. (4856-66, 70)" [86]

It goes without saying that a spur of the iceberg did not pierce the *Titanic's* hull and extend 3.3 feet into the ship like a giant lance resulting in the rupturing of the Fireman's Passage. According to the testimony of Mr. Clement Edwards during the British Wreck Commission hearings, the outer bottom was severely damaged, if not completely removed by the ship's grounding on the iceberg which also resulted in damaging the connective structure between the bottom and the tank top below the Fireman's Passage, resulting in the compromise of the watertight integrity of the Fireman's Passage itself. In this regard, Mr. Clement Edwards testified as follows:

"20726. *I am just coming to that. Assume for the moment that your view about the water coming in there were right, it would be equally consistent if water came in through this skin on the starboard side of the spiral staircase; it would be equally consistent with the inner skin having been wrenched and dislocated by the force of the impact as it would be by actual penetration by the ice?*

- Well, we have had evidence as to the force of the impact; that is, that there was nothing in the nature of what is usually called impact, but that it was a comparatively light sliding blow. I mean that is the whole character of it.

20727. I will put it in another way. I did not use "impact" as applying to the whole area of the ship, but a sufficient strength of collision if you like, at all events, to penetrate the outside plates?

- Yes.

20728. This inner skin on the side of the spiral staircase, I presume, is connected with the outside frame?

- Yes, the floor is, not the side.

20729. So that a blow, an impact, what you will, sufficient to rip the outside plate, if made at a point where there is a connection between the outside skin and the inner skin, Might be sufficient to rip the inside skin and make an aperture?

- Not if the connections are properly arranged, because it is part of the regular practice, Lloyd's Rules, or other, that your boundaries are stronger than your connections. It would be a bad design if it was not so.

20730. I suppose it is because you could not bring yourself to take that view that you have taken the other one?

- Naturally." [87]

It is significant that Mr. Wilding was an employee of Harland and Wolfe and therefore could not agree with Mr. Edwards that his company might have provided a faulty design. It should be noted that the Fireman's Passage led directly to Boiler Room #6 and was a watertight tube that extended through two watertight bulkheads, B and C. Since the Fireman's Passage was watertight and Firemen needed free access from their quarters to the Tank Top Deck boiler rooms, there were no water tight doors in the spiral staircase and only one set of water tight doors leading into Boiler Room #6. We know that Murdoch ordered the watertight compartments closed and that there were also automatic door closing devices that would secure the door in the event the watertight compartment flooded above a level of two feet. Therefore, it cannot be concluded that Boiler Room #6 flooded through the Firemen's Passage. Something else must have happened.

As outlined in David G. Brown's book, *The Last Log of the Titanic*, it was stated that as the ship slid up onto the submerged ledge of the iceberg, the iceberg's center of gravity shifted causing it to hit the side of the *Titanic* [88], simultaneously ripping out the starboard bow bilge keel. The stress of the grounding together with the collision resulted in the rivets popping along the hull as previously described.

It would also appear, from the description given by Barrett, as quoted in Chapter 6, that the damage done in Boiler Room #6 was far more extensive than that to Boiler Room #5 which was compared to that of water emerging from a hose, as opposed to a force which took the water level in Boiler Room #6 to a level of eight feet in a matter of ten minutes.

In conclusion, it would appear almost certain that the *Titanic* hit and rode up onto an underwater ice ledge, causing the iceberg to shift its center of gravity, with the result that it repeatedly bounced off of the side of the starboard hull as Murdoch attempted his "port around" the iceberg. The resulting damage from the collision resulted in a major section of the starboard bow bottom and bilge keel to be removed by the ice as well as creating one, if not more, gashes in the *Titanic's* starboard side below the waterline at the turn of the bilge. This combined damage resulted in a tremendous amount of water, approximately 16,000 tons, flooding the first five watertight compartments in forty minutes which, in turn, led to the bow sinking deep enough to allow water to flow above the watertight bulkhead at Deck E, thereby resulting in the ultimate floundering of what had been hailed as the ship that God Himself could not sink.

CHAPTER 10
WHAT REALLY HAPPENED THAT NIGHT

As previously mentioned, the facts about what happened on the evening of April 14, 2011 and the morning of the next day have always been known. Unfortunately, these facts have been scattered about the ocean floor and hidden away in historical archives for the last ninety-nine years.

Individually, the shattered remains of the once beautiful ship and the testimony of the survivors do not tell the real story of what happened. However, placed in the proper order, these facts can be reassembled into the truth that has been so illusive for all of these years. Therefore, it is important to once again review the key points that have been demonstrated earlier in order to keep a sharp focus on the changes to the "urban legend" that will be made.

If any one thing is clear from reading the testimony of the United States Senate Inquiry and the British Wreck Commission, it is that no one, from Captain Smith on down, believed that the *Titanic* would sink so fast. This helps to explain why the partially filled lifeboats were ordered to the port side gangways to complete the loading process since, unfortunately, it was believed that the lifeboat themselves would buckle and snap in half under the weight of a full complement of people and therefore could not be lowered fifty-eight feet into the sea completely full. Certainly, if Smith, Lightoller and Murdoch had believed that the ship would sink quickly, they would have taken a chance and filled the boats to their maximum capacity at the very start. Unfortunately, for those that died that awful night, the lifeboats did not return and pick up more passengers.

As has already been demonstrated, many issues that had a direct impact upon the rapidity with which the *Titanic* sank, including the fact that when the *Titanic* began to sink, hogging, defined as the bending of the hull resulting from the weight of the water in the bow of the ship had begun with the result that the rivets popped off their heads, loosening the steel plates which, in turn, allowed the sea to enter the ship.[89]

The design of the ship itself also had a major impact on the fact that the ship floundered so rapidly. Whereas the *Titanic* had transverse water tight bulkheads, they did not extend all the way up to "C" Deck and they did not have a watertight tank top. As a result, the *Titanic* started filling up with water, and since she went down by the bow, the water cascaded from one water tight compartment into another because the bulkheads were, for the most part, watertight only up to "E" Deck.

Another cause of the rapid sinking was the failure to extend the double bottom of the *Titanic* completely across the bottom of the ship from the Forepeak Tank through Holds #1, #2, and #3. Unfortunately, it was the single bottom section of the ship that ran aground on a submerged ledge of the iceberg. The resulting collision with the iceberg, produced a force of 1,173,200 foot tons that simply ripped out the bow bilge keel section of the *Titanic*. Even though Boiler Room #6 and #5 had a double hull watertight bottom, they were not impervious to the iceberg as the berg shifted its center of gravity toward the *Titanic*, smacking into the its starboard side shell repeatedly below the water line. As we know, when Boiler Room #6 flooded, the ballgame was over.

Added to the collision was the mistaken belief, expressed by 4th Officer Boxhall who initially reported to Captain Smith after the collision and after a brief visit to the lower decks, that the *Titanic* was not damaged, an opinion that quite possibly led Captain Smith to the decision to restart the engines and proceed "Slow Ahead" in the process forcing enormous amounts of water into the *Titanic* at a much faster rate than would have been the case if she had remained dead in the water.

Finally, there is the issue of exploding boilers. In reality, the ship's boilers exploded right before she floundered. This is an elementary observation to make since the *Titanic* had electric lights that were powered by steam driven electric generators. As the *Titanic* went down by the head and the stern began to rise out of the water, she began to bend and as she did, the rivets that held the tank bottom together began to fail. As the *Titanic's* stern rose higher, the tank top in Boiler Room #4, having bent, began to leak and water began to rise up through the floor as described by George Carvell and Thomas P. Dillion in Chapter 8.

It is a fair assumption that the boilers that fed the electric generators and exploded were in Boiler Rooms #2, as evidenced by Dr. Ballard who photographed intact single ended boilers, now resting on the ocean floor, all of which came from Boiler Room #1. It is interesting to note that no other boilers have ever been discovered in the debris field.

The discovery by John Chatterton and Richie Kohler of complete sections of the tank top that came from Boiler Room #1 also supports the belief that it was these boilers in Boiler Room #2 that exploded and helped to rip out the bottom of the *Titanic* just before she floundered. These two points would therefore indicate that the bending stress of the ship, combined with the exploding boilers, completely separated the tank top and outer bottom in Boiler Room #1 from the side walls of the hull. Without the tank top section support of the hull, as in the case of the melted trusses of the World Trade Center that caused the failure of the outer support walls of the building eighty-nine years later, the tremendously increased stress on the outer walls of the hull led to their failure and the ship tore into two pieces which resulted in two separate sections, the bow and the stern, to sink within a matter of minutes.

Therefore, we can conclude that the exploding boilers added to the series of events that led to the rapid sinking of the *Titanic*, as well as accounting for the rumbling sound, mistakenly reported by some survivors who confused the sound of the ship tearing in half with the imagined sound of the boilers breaking loose from the tank top and smashing their way through the bulkheads to the bow, as they mistakenly perceived the *Titanic* to be standing vertically on her nose and sinking in one piece to the bottom of the Atlantic.

So what really did happen that night? April 14, 1912, the fourth day of the cruse, had been a glorious day, and by now everyone was relaxed and settled into a ship board routine. When Sunday services were held that morning, it must have seemed as though nothing could go wrong. Throughout the cruise, wireless messages had been sent at a furious rate since it seemed that literally everyone on board was teasing their friends and relatives back home with such messages as, "Having a marvelous time, darling. Wish you were here!", little knowing that dark clouds were forming on the distant horizon.

On April 13th, the day before the *Titanic* collision, the ship *Rappahannock* had reported that it had sustained serious damage after hitting an ice flow and on the actual morning of the disaster, two other messages were received, one from the *Carolina* warned of pack ice and icebergs at 42° N, 49° to 51°W and the other from the *Noordam* who was in the same vicinity of the *Carolina* to the same effect. [90]

A multitude of ice warning messages were now being sent by other ships in the area. Around 1:45 P.M., the *Baltic* reported a large ice field located at Latitude 41° 51' N and longitude 49° 52° W. This message was delivered to Captain Smith who gave it to Bruce Ismay, who reportedly put it in his pocket.

It is reported that the message was retrieved by Captain smith and finally returned to the bridge around 7:30 PM. At and around the same time,1:45 PM, a message was received from the *Amerika* reporting ice at 41° 27' N, 50° 8' W, a message which, for some reason, never left the Marconi Room. [91]

As late afternoon and early evening descended on the fated ship,the air temperature dropped from 43° F to 33°F. Before getting ready for dinner, Captain Smith returned to the Bridge because the coordinates 42°N, 47°W were fast approaching and the ship's course would have to be altered to "rounding the corner". The shortest distance between two points is a straight line, however the earth is not flat and therefore navigation techniques would employ the use of spherical trigonometry to plot a great circle across the sea. Rounding the corner is an expression that indicates that the ship's course is being altered from the previous Great Circle Route to a new course, called a rhumb line, which would, in the case of the Titanic, be set to a point south of the Nantucket Shoals Light Vessel.

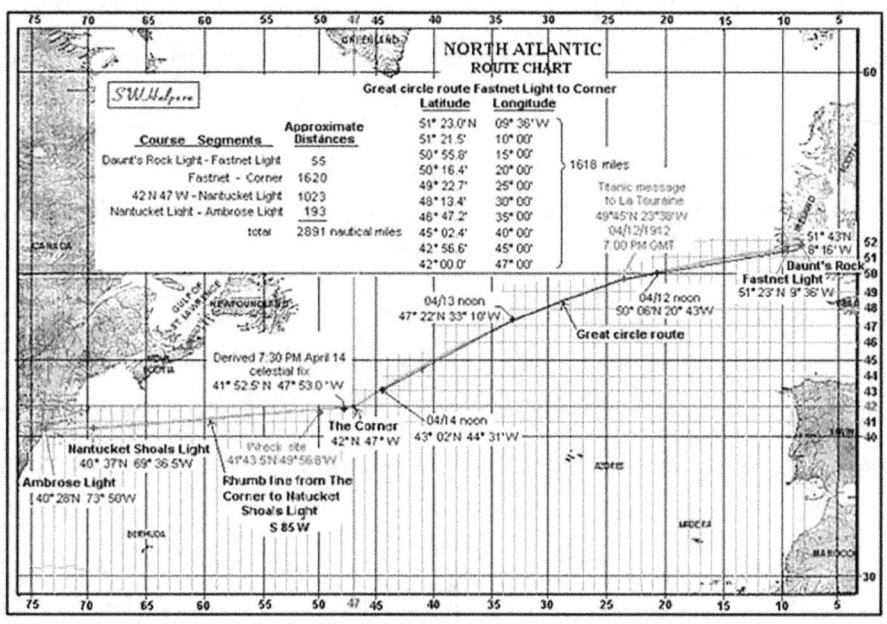

Figure 7 [92]

At approximately 5:45 PM, Quartermaster George T. Rowe took notice of the course change by singing out, the time of the hew heading. In an attempt to avoid ice, apparently Captain Smith had ordered the change of course approximately ten minutes later than was originally scheduled so that the course change would take the *Titanic* a bit more to the south of its original path, little realizing that this final course adjustment would fine tune the ship's trajectory and guarantee that she would collide with the ice flow that was now directly in her path. At 6:00 P.M., Second Officer Lightoller relieved Chief Officer Wilde on the bridge. At approximately, seven-thirty, the *Titanic* received three messages from the ship *Californian* warning of large icebergs at 4° 3' N and 49° 9' W. The Titanic was now only 50 miles from her destiny. [93]

After dinner, at approximately nine in the evening, Captain Smith returned briefly to the bridge and then retired to his cabin and chart room leaving explicit instructions to, "call him if it becomes at all doubtful..." and not only that, but the word be passed on to the crows nest to be watchful for ice. At about 9:40 PM ship's time, a message was received from the *Mesaba* that there are icebergs at 42°N-41°, 25' Long, 49°W-50°, 30' W. For whatever reason, this message was overlooked and never made it to the Bridge. At 10:00 PM ship's time, Second Officer Lightoller was relived by First Officer Murdoch. [94]

At the same time, approximately twenty miles away, the steamer *Californian* was stopped dead in the water and surrounded by ice. At approximately 10:55 PM, the wireless operator of the *Californian* begins his ice warning message only to be interrupted by the wireless operator of the *Titanic* to, "Keep out! Shut up! You're jamming my signal. I'm working Cape race." As a consequence, the *Californian's* ice warning is never received by the *Titanic* and the wireless operator of the *Californian*, retired for the night. It is approximately 11:30 PM.[95]

At 11:40 PM, the *Titanic's* lookouts saw a small iceberg directly in the path of the ship, causing Fleet to ring the bell in the crow's nest three times and telephone the bridge, "Iceberg right ahead." Sixth Officer Moody answered the phone and relayed the message to First Officer Murdoch who ordered helmsman, Robert Hitchens to go "hard-a-starboard" and used the ships Engine Order Telegraph, E.O.T., to instruct the engine room to stop before signaling the engine room to go full astern. Thirty-seven seconds later[96] and traveling at approximately twenty-two knots or 25.317 MPH, the Titanic hit the underground shelf of the iceberg, she listed slightly to port as she ran aground on the starboard side, ripping out her starboard bow peak tank, non-double hull starboard bilge keel sections in holds #1, #2, #3, and the fireman's passage. At the same time, the center of gravity of the iceberg shifted and crashed into the *Titanic's* holing the starboard hull below the waterline in boiler room #6 and #5. Fireman Barrett, in Boiler Room #6, saw a tremendous rush of water into Boiler Room #6 and escaped into Boiler Room #5 as the watertight doors began to close behind him. On the Promenade Deck, Deck A, Edith Russell, walked to her stateroom from the writing room. As she arrived at her door, she heard a bump, turning the door handle to her stateroom, she heard a second bump and as she entered the stateroom, there was a third bump. She immediately walked across the stateroom, went out onto the Promenade Deck and saw what she described as a grey building bumping into the side of the ship. On the Boat Deck, one deck above the Promenade Deck, Quartermaster Alfred Olliver, who was trimming the compass, heard the three bells from Fleet and approaching the Bridge from the port side, observed the iceberg passing astern on the starboard side of the ship. Major Authur G. Peuchen, another First Class passenger, had just arrived in his room when he felt an unusual quivering. In only ten seconds, the fatal damage was done and the iceberg disappeared into the darkness leaving the *Titanic* to suffer her horrible fate.

After the collision, Captain Smith immediately returned to the Bridge where he was informed by Murdoch that the *Titanic* had struck an iceberg. Murdoch went on to say that he attempted a "port around" the iceberg, but it was too late and that after the collision, had closed the watertight doors. Arriving next on the Bridge was Fourth Office Boxhall who was walking from his cabin to the Bridge when Fleet sounded the three warning bells. Captain Smith, First Officer Murdoch and Fourth Officer Boxhall immediately went to the starboard Bridge wing to look for the iceberg. Boxhall described it as being a dark mass about thirty feet above the waterline of the ship. Immediately after that, Boxhall, having taken it upon himself to examine the interior of the *Titanic* could find no damage in the vicinity of the lowest steerage decks in the starboard bow, the area which he thought had been struck. Immediately returning to the bridge, he reported to Captain Smith that there were no indications that the ship had been damaged at all by the collision. Unfortunately for Boxhall, he did not look in the right places. If he had ventured down one more deck, the damage to the ship would have been apparent. As it was, Captain Smith instructed Boxhall to find the carpenter and tell him to "sound" the ship. It was at around this time, 11:52 PM [97] that the Titanic mysteriously started up her engines and steamed "Slow Ahead" for approximately ten to twenty minutes.

Below decks, Lawrence Beesley, a teacher on holiday calmed the nerves of three fellow female passengers by pointing out that the engines were indeed running again and that there was no cause for alarm. To prove his point, he had them place their hand on the bathtub on D deck so they could feel the vibrations of the engines running below.[98] Archibald Gracie, who had felt the Titanic hit the iceberg, dressed and went to the promenade deck, where he observed a couple strolling down the promenade deck walking against the wind, completely oblivious as to what was happening beneath their feet. Since it was a calm night, the presence of the wind could only have meant that the ship was indeed moving forward.[99]

It is presumed by David G. Brown, in *The Last Log Of The Titanic,* that at this point Captain Smith sent a Marconigram to his New York office saying that although the *Titanic* had hit an iceberg, the passengers were safe and that the ship, having changed course, was steaming to Halifax, Nova Scotia.[100] It should be noted that this fact was not testified to by Harold S. Bride, the surviving Marconi wireless operator on the *Titanic* at the United States Disaster Hearings or the British Wreck Commissioner Inquiry.

Oddly enough, a similar telegram was sent by Phillips to his family and later on, eighteen hours after the ship had sunk, the ship's owners, the White Star Line, sent a similar telegram to US Senator James Hughes. Henry Aldridge and Sons in Devizes, Wilts, auctioned off the Hughes telegram in September 2006 for ten thousand pounds sterling. Also for the record, railroad trains were actually dispatched to Halifax to pick up the *Titanic* survivors and then later recalled when the news of the sinking became known.

Whereas, the true author of this Marconigram will never be known, Captain Smith would have been the logical person to send it, reporting the condition of his ship immediately after the collision with the iceberg to the White Star Line. The fact that the *Titanic* resumed steaming after the collision can only give credence to the theory that the telegram was sent and the ship was trying to get to Halifax.

Elsewhere on the ship, Boxhall found the carpenter, John Hutchinson who was on his way to the bridge to tell Captain Smith, "The ship is making water."[101] Boxhall was also told by Hutchinson that the mail hold was filling rapidly. Upon investigating the mail room himself, Boxhall observed mail bags floating about and returned to the Bridge, to tell Captain Smith what he had seen. At around midnight, Captain Smith and ship designer, Thomas Andrews, quickly inspected the damage in the Peak Tank, Holds #1, #2, #3 and Boiler Room #6, an inspection that made it clear that the *Titanic* would sink very quickly. Returning to the Bridge, the Captain ordered the engines to stop for the last time. Murdoch responded to his order by using the ships Engine Order Telegraph, E.O.T., and signaled the engine room, "Astern Slow" and finally "All Stop". Resigned to the fate of his ship, Captain Smith instructed the crew to uncover the lifeboats and bring the passengers to the Boat Deck. By this time, the ship was flooded almost to the waterline at the bow, thirty-four feet, seven inches above the keel and the Squash Court, thirty-two feet above the keel was flooded with two feet of water. At nine minutes after twelve midnight on the morning of April 15, 1912, Captain Smith entered the wireless room and instructed the operators to send out the CQD distress message and their position, which was 41° 46'N, 50° 14' W. [102]

There was no emergency alarm sounded as shown in the 1953 film, *Titanic*; however, the crew of the Titanic quietly began to collect the passengers telling them to report to the boat deck, to dress warmly and to wear their life perservers. It is believed that this was done to prevent widespread panic aboard the ship.

As soon as the *Titanic's* wireless operator Phillips sent out the CQD, he began receiving replies from various ships, the *Olympic, Mount Temple, Frankfort, Birma, Baltic, Virginian* and the *Carpathia*. Even though the *Mount Temple* was closest to the Titanic, the *Carpathia* was the ship that arrived first at the wreck site several hours later. The *Titanic's* band played music on A Deck as the water inside the *Titanic* rose to a level eight feet seven inches above the waterline or forty-three feet above the keel and chased the firemen from their sleeping quarters in the bow as the gathered on the well deck.

By approximately a quarter to one in the morning, the *Titanic* lifeboats began to be lowered and Boxhall started firing emergency distress rockets into the sky to draw the attention of a ship that he saw off in the distance, exciting, however, no response. A frustrated Captain Smith instructed Boxhall to also uses the Morse Lamp to contact the ship, but again no response. Off in the distance, perhaps ten to twenty miles away, officers of the *Californian* observed a large passenger ship approach and then watched a total of eight rockets shoot into the sky. Using their Morse Lamp, they tried to contact the ship and got no reply. Eventually, they watched the ship apparently sail away and vanish. They would not find out what happened to the *Titanic* until the following morning when their Marconi operator woke up and turned on his set. [103]

Unfortunately, there was a common belief, apparently shared by many of the *Titanic's* officers who were loading the lifeboats that the lifeboats could not be lowered to the sea, a distance of approximately fifty-eight feet, fully loaded because they would buckle and snap into due to the weight of the passengers. Therefore, the majority of the initial lifeboats launched, were partially filled. It is believed that Lightoller and Captain Smith fully expected the lifeboats to return to the *Titanic* and fill up the partially filled lifeboats using the forward gangway.

Lifeboat #7 was the first to be lowered. It could carry sixty-five people but only twenty-eight were on board. Lightoller had instructed the lifeboats to be rowed to the port side gangway doors in the bow of the ship where more passengers could be taken on board the lifeboats. Lifeboat #6 on the port side was the next lifeboat to be launched with only twenty-eight people on board. The appalling lack of passengers continued as lifeboats #5, #3, #1 and #8 were lowered into the sea all partially filled. [104]

At 1:15 PM, it is reported that Captain Smith, using a megaphone, began to hail the partially filled lifeboats, instructing them to return to the ship. Unfortunately, none return. The water was now up to the ship's name on the bow and she had begun to list to port. [105] It is assumed today that the water was now entering the Titanic on the port side through the open gangway doors and at 1:20 PM, because of hogging, water began to flood Boiler Room #4 from the tank top up.

Between 1:20 AM and 1:55 AM, as the bow of the ship sank further and further into the sea, lifeboats #2, #4, #9, #10, #11 #12, #13, #14, #13, #15, #16 and collapsible lifeboat C were launched. The officers, realizing by now that the *Titanic* would flounder soon, started to fill the lifeboats with more and more people; however, when all was said and done, none were loaded to their maximum capacity.

At 1:45 A.M., the *Carpathia* received the last broken message from the *Titanic*, "Engine room full up to boilers ..." By two that morning, with the water only ten feet below the Promenade Deck, Lightoller filled and lowered Collapsible Lifeboat D. At 2:10 AM, Captain Smith released the wireless operators, Bride and Phillips, from their duties, but Phillips continued to transmit messages. After bellowing to his crew, "It's every man for himself.", Captain Smith was last seen returning to the Bridge. It was now approximately 2:17 PM. The ships band, that had been playing ragtime for most of the night, switched to hymns during the last remaining minutes. Whereas some survivors recalled hearing the hymn "Autumn", others reported hearing, "Nearer My God To Thee", and still others recalled hearing "Abide With Me". Regardless, after having retreated to the Boat Deck the band finally stopped playing and along with the others that remained aboard the doomed ship, would vanish beneath the waves and into the pages of history.[106]

Inside the mighty *Titanic*, the weight of the water in the bow and the weight of the propellers and engines in the stern had been fighting each other since the collision, with the result that the ship had bent like an archer's bow, the stern having been raised higher and higher out of the water as the forecastle head sank beneath the waves. The ship's bottom and tank top were failing under the tremendous bending stress, referred to as "hogging"; as the rivets began to pop, loosening the steel plates and allowing water to rapidly fill the ship's remaining watertight compartments. The boilers at the stern of the ship, in particular, Boiler Room #2 were lit and were supplying steam at 183 psi to the generators that were keeping the lights burning throughout the ship.

Having been released by Captain Smith, Lightoller had gone to Collapsible Lifeboat B on the port side of the *Titanic*. The collapsible boat had been cut from its lashings and had fallen from its position on top of the Officer's quarters onto the Boat Deck upside down. Lightoller walked to the starboard side and observed First Officer Murdoch for the last time, attempting to get the Collapsible lifeboat A onto the davits so it could be lowered into the sea. As Lightoller returned to the port side, the *Titanic* took a plunge and a wave washed Lightoller and the Collapsible Lifeboat B into the sea.

Lightoller tried to swim away from the ship, but was immediately sucked against a wire mesh that covered the throat of a blower on the *Titanic* deck, an upside "J" tubular air vent that faced forward collecting fresh air from the forward motion of the ship, directing it into the depths of the decks below. As the water gurgled down the blower, Lightoller was pinned against the wire grating by the water pressure and was eventually blown toward the surface by the inevitable warm rush of air coming from an exploding boiler. First Class passenger, Archibald Grace who was also attempting to leave the ship, jumped with the force of a wave behind him to the hurricane deck where he frantically held onto a railing as the bow sank beneath the waves, taking him with it into a cauldron of hot swirling water from which , after he let go of the railing, surfaced next to an overturned collapsible lifeboat. Lightoller also found himself next to the same upside-down Collapsible Lifeboat B and climbed aboard just as the number one funnel (smokestack) of the *Titanic* fell into the sea narrowly missing him and pushing Collapsible Lifeboat B approximately 150 feet away from the rapidly sinking vessel.

When the water rose above the bridge and began to flood the boat deck, the surviving passengers and crew, starting to become desperate, retreated toward the perceived safety of the stern of the ship. As the bow sank and the stern began to rise at a faster pace, two things happen almost simultaneously: the ship's hogging allowed water into Boiler Rooms #2 at a rapid rate which caused the explosions of the steam filled boilers in the latter and the electric generators, in response to the explosions, stopped working, causing the electricity to go off as sections of the tank top of Boiler Room #1, weakened by the boiler explosions and hogging of the ship, suddenly ripped loose from the verticle shell of the *Titanic* and sank along with the single ended boilers to the ocean floor. In the darkness, the port and starboard hull began to rip apart, producing a horrible rumbling sound described by many survivors and officers of the *Titanic*. It is approximately 2:18 A.M, April 15, 1912.[107]

In the darkness, the bow section of the *Titanic* disappeared into the depths of the sea leaving the stern sticking almost vertically into the sky. The survivors in the lifeboats watched in silence as the black image of the stern started to make its final plunge into the sea. Some of the survivors compared the screams of the poor souls during those final moments to that of the roar of a crowd at a ball game when a batter hits a home run. It was approximately 2:20 A.M. when the stern section sank beneath the surface of the sea, never to be seen again until September 1, 1985 when the resting place of the *Titanic* was finally discovered by Dr. Robert Ballard.[108]

CHAPTER ELEVEN
UNINTENDED CONSEQUENCES

Now that we have examined the sinking of the *Titanic* based on the testimony of those that survived the terrible disaster, we will explore, in the final chapter of this book, the "unintended consequences" that resulted from decisions that were made long before the *Titanic* became a physical reality as well as the actions of the crew on the fateful night. It will be up to the reader to make the final judgment as to the degree of importance the factors presented, separately or collectively, played in producing the "unintended consequences" that would sink the mighty *Titanic*. To that end, let us review each in turn.

Bulkhead Design

A decision was made by Harland and Wolff to equip the ship with fifteen transverse watertight bulkheads that would create sixteen watertight compartments. The design also called for bring bulkheads #2, #10, #11, #12, #13, #14, and #15 to D deck and bulkheads #3, #4, #5, #6, #7, #8, and #9 only to E deck. Unfortunately, when the *Titanic* hit the iceberg, the first five watertight compartments flooded, thus allowing the bow of the ship to sink to a level that would allow the water to flood over the top of Transverse Bulkheads #3, #4, #5, #6, #7, #8 and #9. This cascading effect from one watertight compartment to another was the primary cause for the sinking of the *Titanic*. What would have happened if the transverse bulkheads extended to C deck and had a watertight tank top?

Titanic's Double Bottom

A decision was made by Harland and Wolff to install a double bottom that would allow for the outer skin of the ship to be pierced without flooding the interior of the ship because of the construction of a second interior watertight skin called the "tank top". The distance that separated the outer skin from the inner tank top was approximately five feet throughout. This area was also divided into separate sections that were used for ballast and water storage.

The decision to have a double bottom however, did not call for a complete double bottom in the bow or the stern of the ship or more importantly, on the starboard bow section of the ship. Unfortunately, the *Titanic* hit an underwater ledge of the iceberg on the starboard bow, and as a result, in ten seconds, the iceberg pierced the Peek Tank, ripped out the starboard bilge keel of the first four watertight compartments, smashed through the Firemen's Passage, and at the same time, shifted the center of gravity of the iceberg, thereby making it crash into the starboard shell of the *Titanic* below the waterline, with the result that Boiler Room #6 and #5 were flooded. What would have happened if the watertight double bottom extended 100 % throughout the bottom of the ship?

Lifeboats

It is safe to say that if, the *Titanic* had been equipped with enough lifeboats for everyone on board, the catastrophe might have been averted. Unfortunately, the number of lifeboats with which the *Titanic* was outfitted, was the result of a guideline established by the Board of Trade, Marine Department. Unfortunately, these rules, which were drafted in 1894 were not modified until after the *Titanic* sank.

The failure to review and modify the lifeboat rules was primarily due to the fact that not that many people died because of sinking ships. In fact at that time, traveling by steam ship was considered to be the safest mode of travel. Secondly, as the ships grew in size, it was believed that their construction and overall design made them safer ships that the ones that had be built earlier.

In a telephone discussion I had with David G. Brown, David pointed out that the ships of this time period traveled similar routes crossing the Atlantic and in the event of danger, could assist one another. Therefore, the lifeboats were to be used as "sea taxies" to transport people from the sinking ship to the rescuing ship. As a result, the conclusion was to simply do nothing since the Board of Trade refused to place what they considered to be unnecessary regulations on the industry.

From 1894 through 1912, the Board of Trade, Marine Department only had provisions for lifeboats for ships that went up to ten-thousand tons. Any ship that was larger that that still had the same lifeboat requirements as a ten-thousand ton vessel, which was why the *Titanic*, four and a half times bigger than that, with a gross tonnage of 46,328 tons, was only required to have sixteen lifeboats.

Actually, the *Titanic* exceeded the Board of Trade requirements by having two emergency lifeboats, fourteen wooden lifeboats and four Engelhard collapsible lifeboats for a total of twenty lifeboats with a total capacity capable of accommodating 1,178 passengers. Unfortunately, the *Titanic* was caring 2,340 passengers and crew. What would have happened if the Board of Trade, Marine Division had kept up with the ever increasing tonnage of the passenger ships and had made it mandatory for each ship to carry enough lifeboats for all passengers and crew on board the ship?

It is difficult to answer this question since simply having a seat on a lifeboat does not mean that you will survive a sinking ship. As it was on the night of April 15, 1912, the crew did not have enough time to launch their twenty lifeboats and two collapsible lifeboats were washed overboard. If they had forty lifeboats, would the outcome have been any different? The answer is probably not. The "unintended consequence" of the *Titanic* lifeboat tragedy was the changing of the rules that stipulated the number of lifeboats a ship should carry in such a way that everyone could be guaranteed a seat in case of evacuation. In all actuality however, this means very little under certain circumstances. Simply put, having a seat on a lifeboat does not necessarily mean that you will survive.

Titanic's Speed

Unfortunately, there has been a lot of speculation over the years that Captain Smith was reckless and did not slow down when he received ice warnings. Hindsight being twenty-twenty, we know that he should have. Others have speculated that there was some form of collusion between Ismay and Smith, with Smith yielding to the demands of Ismay to disregard the ice warnings and plow into the ice filled waters for the sake of making a speed record.

In all actuality, both assertions are incorrect. Quoting from The British Wreck Commission,

"It was shown that for many years past, indeed, for a quarter of a century or more, the practice of liners using this track when in the vicinity of ice at night had been in clear weather to keep the course, to maintain the speed and to trust to a sharp look-out to enable them to avoid the danger. This practice, it was said, had been justified by experience, no casualties having resulted from it. I accept the evidence as to the practice and as to the immunity from casualties which is said to have accompanied it. But the event has proved the practice to be bad. Its root is probably to be found in competition and in the desire of the public for quick passages rather than in the judgment of navigators. But unfortunately experience appeared to justify it. In these circumstances I am not able to blame Captain Smith. He had not the experience which his own misfortune has afforded to those whom he has left behind, and he was doing only that which other skilled men would have done in the same position. It was suggested at the bar that he was yielding to influences which ought not to have

affected him; that the presence of Mr. Ismay on board and the knowledge which he perhaps had of a conversation between Mr. Ismay and the Chief Engineer {Bell} at Queenstown about the speed of the ship and the consumption of coal probably induced him to neglect precautions which he would otherwise have taken. But I do not believe this. The evidence shows that he was not trying to make any record passage or indeed any exceptionally quick passage. He was not trying to please anybody, but was exercising his own discretion in the way he thought best. He made a mistake, a very grievous mistake, but one in which, in face of the practice and of past experience, negligence cannot be said to have had any part; and in the absence of negligence it is, in my opinion, impossible to fix Captain Smith with blame. It is, however, to be hoped that the last has been heard of the practice and that for the future it will be abandoned for what we now know to be more prudent and wiser measures. What was a mistake in the case of the "Titanic" would without doubt be negligence in any similar case in the future." [109]

Be that as it may, there is still the "unintended consequence", of having struck the iceberg because the speed of the *Titanic* was not reduced. One would therefore ask, would the *Titanic* have sunk if she had reduced her speed, thereby giving the lookouts more time to announce the ice warning, and thus giving the *Titanic* more than thirty-seven seconds to miss the iceberg completely? The answer is maybe.

Lookout Binoculars

Much has been said about the fact that the lookouts did not have binoculars. It has been suggested that the "unintended consequence" of the lookouts not having binoculars, led to the fatal collision. For those who have used binoculars, however, it is quite clear that one does not see anything except that which is in their field of vision. The truth of the matter is that binoculars are only good for getting "up close and personal" with the object in question not for wide angle scanning, in particular at night. The lookouts were trained to look for icebergs with their naked eyes as well as to keep an eye out for other factors, such as suddenly noting that something was blocking the lookout's ability to see the stars on the horizon, which would suggest there was possibly an iceberg in their path. This type of observation is best done without the aid of binoculars. Therefore it would be doubtful that if Fleet did have binoculars, he would have seen the iceberg any sooner, and that if he did, it would have been due to an incredible stroke of good fortune.

Blue Icebergs and Flat Calm

It was reported by Fleet and Lightoller that the iceberg was dark in color and Lightoller used the term "turned turtle" meaning that the iceberg had recently flipped a submerged section of its mass to the surface. The "unintended consequence" of the opaque, or blue appearance of the iceberg was that it was not observed until it was too late. Added to that were the lack of waves, it being a moonless night with a sea described as "flat calm", waves which, had they been splashing against the iceberg, might have served as a warning of its existence.

One could only ask, what would have happened that night if the iceberg had been white and if there had been a breeze that would have created waves at the base of the berg? Since there was no moon to illuminate the white iceberg, nor were there waves, we will never know the answer to these questions with the result that they must be filed in the "IF "IFS" AND "ANDS" WERE POTS AND PANS" category.

Hitting The Iceberg Head On

Many have considered it a mistake for Murdock to have attempted a "port around" the iceberg and believe that, if the *Titanic* would have hit the berg head on, the ship would not have floundered. The "unintended consequence" in this case was that the "port around" led to the hitting of a submerged ledge of the iceberg which ripped out the starboard bilge keel.

Since the birthing quarters for the firemen and the third class passengers were both located in the bow of the ship and considering that it was 11:40 PM, it is very likely that there would have been a tremendous loss of life if the *Titanic* had collided with the berg head on at a speed of approximately 22 knots. There would also have been causalities throughout the ship as the *Titanic* came to an abrupt halt, throwing everyone around the ship like rag dolls. In the end, however, the *Titanic* would have probably remained afloat long enough for rescue ships to save all of the remaining passengers.

Boxhall's Report To Captain Smith

Fourth Officer Boxhall was approaching the bridge when he heard the three warning bells sounded by the lookout, Fleet. Arriving on the bridge, Boxhall, along with Captain Smith and First Officer Murdoch went to the starboard bridge-wing and observed the iceberg disappearing into the darkness. Boxhall then took it upon himself to investigate the starboard bow section below decks and immediately returned to the bridge and told Captain Smith that he saw no damage to the ship. Interestingly enough, it was at this moment that the *Titanic* resumed its progress, steaming at a speed of "Slow Ahead" for approximately ten to twenty minutes. It has been suggested by David Brown in his book *The Last Log Of The Titanic* that during this time, Captain Smith sent a Marconigram to the White Star office in New York saying that the *Titanic* had hit an iceberg, all passengers were safe and that they were heading to Halifax.

The "unintended consequence" of Boxhall's report to Captain Smith was that it could have made Captain Smith start up the engines and begin to steam forward once again. Because the *Titanic* was moving forward with a substantial hole in her starboard bow, the forward motion of the ship would have forced vast quantities of water into the first five compartments at a faster rate than would have been the case if the ship had remained motionless after the collision. As it was, the rapid flooding of the first five compartments resulted in the loss of precious time on the surface and led to the sinking of the mighty ship before rescue ships arrived. What would have happened if Boxhall had not told Captain Smith that all was well?

On a side bar, it was reported by David G. Brown in his book, *The Last Log Of The Titanic*, that Second Officer Lightoller was the Captain of a Royal Navy ship during World War I and rammed a German U-Boat. The bow of Lightoller's ship was badly damaged, but he made it safely back to port by steaming "backwards".[110] Perhaps this is an example of a positive "unintended consequence" that came out of the *Titanic* tragedy.

The *Californian*

The "unintended consequence" of having Marconi operator Phillips tell the *Californian* Marconi operator to "Shut up...DDD...DDD...I'm working Cape Race,"[111] led to the decision of the radio operator on the *Californian* to retire for the night without telling Phillips that they were stopped dead in the ice at approximately twenty miles North of the *Titanic*. After the collision, the *Californian's* officers did not respond to the *Titanic's* distress rockets and watched as the *Titanic* sank, thinking it was sailing away from them and disappearing over the horizon. Because the radio operator had turned his set off and gone to bed, he did not respond to the *Titanic's* distress call CQD or SOS. I think everyone would agree that if the *Californian* had responded to the *Titanic*, there would have been no loss of life.

Boiler Explosions

One of the many hotly disputed topics of the *Titanic* disaster is the issue of boiler explosions prior to and at the time of, the floundering of the *Titanic*. As discussed in Chapter 8, there is ample evidence that there were several explosions immediately prior to the *Titanic* going to the bottom. Many conclude that, since the steam in the boilers was vented earlier on, as Murdoch and Lightoller were first loading the lifeboats - a fact that

Hollywood likes to dramatize in their films of the disaster - there was no steam left in the boilers and therefore, there could have been no explosions. The fact of the matter is that steam that was being vented early on in the sinking drama was only from Boiler Room #6 and #5.

Everyone seems to forget that the lights of the Titanic remained on, perhaps until five minutes before she broke apart and floundered. These lights were powered by steam driven generators that required 183 psi to maintain the power to the lights. Due to the weight of the water in the bow vs. the propellers and heavy equipment in the stern, the integrity of the tank top failed and the water rapidly flooded Boiler Room #2, with the result that they exploded and blew out the bottom of the ship, leading to the weakening of the *Titanic's* shell and the ultimate ripping apart of the mighty ship. The "unintended consequence" of keeping the steam in the boilers in Boiler Rooms #2 in order to keep the lights on, was the unexpected explosions that helped to account for the rapid sinking of the *Titanic*. If there had been no explosions of the boilers, what would have happened to the ship? Would she have broken apart on the surface or would she have remained intact, floating long enough for the *Carpathia* to rescue all of the passengers and crew?

In conclusion, it is evident that there was no one single event that caused the sinking of the *Titanic*, but rather a combination of conditions, all of which, working in conjunction, led to the ultimate "unintended consequence", which was the sinking of the largest passenger ship in the world on the evening of April 14, 1912 and the morning of April 15, 1912.

These unfortunate decisions, the design of the ship's watertight transverse bulkheads, regulation that led to the lack of sufficient lifeboats to save all of the passengers and crew, the calm sea, the failure to slow down as the *Titanic* entered the ice region, the blue iceberg, the decision by Murdoch to "port around" the iceberg, Fourth Officer Boxhall's unfortunate statement to Captain Smith that the ship was not damaged, the decision of Captain Smith to proceed "Slow Ahead" with a gaping hole in the starboard bow, the failure of the *Californian* to come to the aid of the *Titanic* and the rapid break up of the *Titanic* on the surface were all resulted in an "unintended consequences" that simply could not be overcome.

Ironically, if one or two of the decisions that were made before the *Titanic* was constructed had been changed, for example having the watertight transverse bulkheads extend to C deck with a watertight tank top, having enough lifeboats for everyone, or if the *Californian* had responded to the *Titanic's* cry for help, the tragedy could possibly have been easily averted.

If some of the decisions that were made when the *Titanic* hit the iceberg had been modified, for example, hitting the iceberg "head on" without trying to execute a "port around" or if Fourth Officer Boxhall had reported the damage correctly to Captain Smith when he made his first report that there was no damage, perhaps Captain Smith would not have started steaming "Slow Ahead" with a mortally wounded ship and the mighty Titanic would not have floundered as quickly as she did.

In retrospect, you could say that the beginning of the *Titanic* disaster actually began in 1894 when the Board of Trade, Marine Division failed to keep up with the increasing sizes of the passenger ships thereby increasing the number of lifeboats accordingly. Inadequate engineering design considerations for tank tops for the watertight compartments of the *Titanic* also contributed to sealing the fate of those that died on the morning of April 15, 1912, making the fate of the ship predestined, doomed before she was ever launched.

A final point to consider is Divine Providence. When I was a child, my grandmother, a strong Baptist God fearing woman, would often remark, "When it's your time to go, there is nothing in this whole wide world that will keep you from meeting your Maker." Unfortunately for those 1,503 souls that were lost on the *Titanic* on that horrible night, April 15, 1912, it would seem that their time to meet their Maker was at hand. May they rest in peace.

THE END

ACKNOWLEDGEMENTS

Titanic, Unintended Consequences has been locked up inside of my mind for many years. It has only been recently that I have had the time to organize what I have been thinking and then, try to put it on paper. Since I was born in 1946, I have no first hand knowledge of the *Titanic* disaster other that what I can read from those who have gone before me both in a literal and publishing sense.

It is to these people to whom I own a great deal of thanks. This list includes Dr. Robert Ballard who found the *Titanic* wreck and graciously allowed me to quote the timeline in his book, *The Discovery Of The Titanic*. I would like to thank Samuel Halpern, an Encyclopedia Titanica member since March 22, 2003, for giving me his permission to quote his published work. Mr. Halpern's insight into the *Titanic* disaster and drawings are second to none and I would highly recommend his work to anyone looking for data on this subject. A world of thanks to Mr. Ed Walker for allowing me to use his painting of the *Titanic* for the book cover. Last but not least is Mr. David G. Brown. Mr. Brown's, *"The Last Log Of The Titanic"*, is a fresh new look on the *Titanic* that breaks away from the ordinary and plows new ground as to what really happened that night. Thanks for the phone calls David, you were very inspirational and I wish you well with your new book *Titanic Myths, Titanic Truths*.

Needless to say, without the permission of Dr. Ballard, Samuel Halpern, Ed Walker and David G. Brown to cite and use their work, I could not have completed my book. Thank you gentlemen.

BIBLIOGRAPHY

Ballard, Robert D., *The Discovery Of The Titanic,* New York: Warner Communications, A Warner/Madison Press Book, 1987.

Everett, Marshall, *Wreck and Sinking of the Titanic,* L.H. Walter, 1912.

Halpern, Samuel, *Titanic's Hidden Decks*, http://www.encyclopedia-titanica.org/titanic-hidden-deck.html.

Halpern, Samuel, *Somewhere About 12 Square Feet,* http://www.Titanicology.com/MyonlinePublications.html.

Halpern, Samuel, Titanic's Prime Mover – *An Examination of Propulsion and Power, Auxiliary Steam Supply and the Electrical Power Plant,* http://www.encyclopedia-titanica.org/titanic_prime_mover.html

Kuntz, Tom, *The Titanic Disaster Hearings: The Official Transcripts of the 1912 Senate Investigation,* Pocket Books, 1998.

Marshall, Logan, *Sinking of the Titanic and Great Sea Disasters,* L.T.Myers, 1912.

Matsen, Brad, *TITANIC'S LAST SECRETS,* New York: Hachette Book Group USA, 2008.

McCluskie, Tom, *The Wall Chart Of The Titanic,* San Diego, CA, Thunder Bay Press, 1998.

Mowbrey, Jay Henry, *SINKING OF THE TITANIC,* Harrisberg, PA, Geo. W. Berton, 1912.

The Titanic Reports, The 1912 Inquiries by the US Senate and the British Wreck Commission, St. Petersburg, FL, Red and Black Publishers.

Winocour, Jack, *The story of the TITANIC as told by its survivors,* New York, Dover Publications, Inc., 1960.

Endnotes

1. Dr. Robert D. Ballard, <u>The Discovery Of The Titanic</u> (Warner Books Inc., 1987) 220.
2. Ballard 220.
3. Ballard 220.
4. Ballard 220.
5. Ballard 220-221.
6. Ballard 221.
7. Ballard 221.
8. Ballard 221.
9. Ballard 221.
10. Ballard 221.
11. Ballard 222.
12. Ballard 221-222.
13. <u>The Titanic Reports</u> (Red and Black Publishers) 42.
14. *"Titanic Inquiry Project"* (http//www.titanicinquiry.org).
15. *"Titanic Inquiry Project"* (http//www.titanicinquiry.org).
16. Edith Russell, Interviewed by the BBC on April 14, 1970, http://www.bbc.co.uk/archive/titanic/5051.shtml?all=1&id=5051
17. *"Titanic Inquiry Project"* (http//www.titanicinquiry.org).
18. *"Titanic Inquiry Project"* (http//www.titanicinquiry.org).
19. *"Titanic Inquiry Project"* (http//www.titanicinquiry.org).
20. *"Titanic Inquiry Project"* (http//www.titanicinquiry.org).
21. *"Titanic Inquiry Project"* (http//www.titanicinquiry.org).
22. *"Titanic Inquiry Project"* (http//www.titanicinquiry.org).
23. *"Titanic Inquiry Project"* (http//www.titanicinquiry.org).
24. *"Titanic Inquiry Project"* (http//www.titanicinquiry.org).

25 David G. Brown, The Last Log Of The Titanic (International Marine, 2001) 108.
26 Titanic Reports (Red and Black Publishers) 42-46.
27 Samuel Halpern, *Titanic's Hidden Decks*, http://www.encyclopedia-titanica.org/titanic-hidden-deck.html.
28 Samuel Halpern, *Somewhere About 12 Square Feet*, http://www.Titanicology.com/MyonlinePublications.html.
29 Titanic Reports (Red and Black Publishers) 44.
30 Titanic Reports (Red and Black Publishers) 100.
31 Samuel Halpern, *Somewhere About 12 Square Feet*, http://www.Titanicology.com/MyonlinePublications.html.
32 *"Titanic Inquiry Project"* (http//www.titanicinquiry.org).
33 *"Titanic Inquiry Project"* (http//www.titanicinquiry.org).
34 Samuel Halpern, *Titanic's Hidden Decks*, http://www.encyclopedia-titanica.org/titanic-hidden-deck.html.
35 Samuel Halpern, *Titanic's Hidden Decks*, http://www.encyclopedia-titanica.org/titanic-hidden-deck.html.
36 Samuel Halpern, *Titanic's Hidden Decks*, http://www.encyclopedia-titanica.org/titanic-hidden-deck.html.
37 Samuel Halpern, *Titanic's Prime Mover – An Examination of Propulsion and Power, Auxiliary Steam Supply and the Electrical Power Plant*, http://www.encyclopedia-titanica.org/titanic_prime_mover.html
38 Samuel Halpern, *Titanic's Prime Mover – An Examination of Propulsion and Power, Auxiliary Steam Supply and the Electrical Power Plant*, http://www.encyclopedia-titanica.org/titanic_prime_mover.html
39 *"Titanic Inquiry Project"* (http//www.titanicinquiry.org).
40 *"Titanic Inquiry Project"* (http//www.titanicinquiry.org).
41 *"Titanic Inquiry Project"* (http//www.titanicinquiry.org).
42 *"Titanic Inquiry Project"* (http//www.titanicinquiry.org).

43 *"Titanic Inquiry Project"* (http//www.titanicinquiry.org).

44 *"Titanic Inquiry Project"* (http//www.titanicinquiry.org).

45 *"Titanic Inquiry Project"* (http//www.titanicinquiry.org).

46 *"Titanic Inquiry Project"* (http//www.titanicinquiry.org).

47 *"Titanic Inquiry Project"* (http//www.titanicinquiry.org).

48 *"Titanic Inquiry Project"* (http//www.titanicinquiry.org).

49 Samuel Halpern, *Somewhere About 12 Square Feet*, http://www.Titanicology.com/MyonlinePublications.html.

50 *"Titanic Inquiry Project"* (http//www.titanicinquiry.org).

51 *"Titanic Inquiry Project"* (http//www.titanicinquiry.org).

52 David G. Brown, The Last Log Of The Titanic (International Marine, 2001) 131.

53 *"Titanic Inquiry Project"* (http//www.titanicinquiry.org).

54 Samuel Halpern, *Somewhere About 12 Square Feet*, http://www.Titanicology.com/MyonlinePublications.html.

55 David G. Brown, The Last Log Of The Titanic (International Marine, 2001) 106.

56 *"Titanic Inquiry Project"* (http//www.titanicinquiry.org).

57 *"Titanic Inquiry Project"* (http//www.titanicinquiry.org).

58 *"Titanic Inquiry Project"* (http//www.titanicinquiry.org).

59 *"Titanic Inquiry Project"* (http//www.titanicinquiry.org).

60 *"Titanic Inquiry Project"* (http//www.titanicinquiry.org).

61 *"Titanic Inquiry Project"* (http//www.titanicinquiry.org).

62 *"Titanic Inquiry Project"* (http//www.titanicinquiry.org).

63 *"Titanic Inquiry Project"* (http//www.titanicinquiry.org).

64 *"Titanic Inquiry Project"* (http//www.titanicinquiry.org).

65 *"Titanic Inquiry Project"* (http//www.titanicinquiry.org).

66 Ballard, 221.

67 *"Titanic Inquiry Project"* (http//www.titanicinquiry.org).

68. Brown 210.
69. *"Titanic Inquiry Project"* (http//www.titanicinquiry.org).
70. *"Titanic Inquiry Project"* (http//www.titanicinquiry.org).
71. *"Titanic Inquiry Project"* (http//www.titanicinquiry.org).
72. *"Titanic Inquiry Project"* (http//www.titanicinquiry.org).
73. *"Titanic Inquiry Project"* (http//www.titanicinquiry.org).
74. *"Titanic Inquiry Project"* (http//www.titanicinquiry.org).
75. *"Titanic Inquiry Project"* (http//www.titanicinquiry.org).
76. *"Titanic Inquiry Project"* (http//www.titanicinquiry.org).
77. *"Titanic Inquiry Project"* (http//www.titanicinquiry.org).
78. Marshall Everett, <u>Wreck and Sinking of the TITANIC</u> (L. H. WALTERS, 1912) 82.
79. *"Titanic Inquiry Project"* (http//www.titanicinquiry.org).
80. *"Titanic Inquiry Project"* (http//www.titanicinquiry.org).
81. *"Titanic Inquiry Project"* (http//www.titanicinquiry.org).
82. *"Titanic Inquiry Project"* (http//www.titanicinquiry.org).
83. *"Titanic Inquiry Project"* (http//www.titanicinquiry.org).
84. *"Titanic Inquiry Project"* (http//www.titanicinquiry.org).
85. Brown 105.
86. *"Titanic Inquiry Project"* (http//www.titanicinquiry.org).
87. *"Titanic Inquiry Project"* (http//www.titanicinquiry.org).
88. Brown 88.
89. Brown 148.
90. Ballard 220.
91. Ballard 221.
92. Samuel Halpern, *Keeping Track Of A Maiden Voyage,* http://www.encyclopedia-titanica.org/keeping_track.html.
93. Ballard 221.
94. Ballard 221.

95 Ballard 221.
96 Ballard 221.
97 Brown 131.
98 Brown 138.
99 Brown 139.
100 Brown 131.
101 Brown 130.
102 Ballard 221.
103 Ballard 221-222.
104 Ballard 222.
105 Ballard 222.
106 Ballard 222.
107 Ballard 222.
108 Ballard 222.
109 *"Titanic Inquiry Project"* (http//www.titanicinquiry.org).
110 Brown 196.
111 Brown 43.

www.ingramcontent.com/pod-product-compliance
Lightning Source LLC
LaVergne TN
LVHW051838080426
835512LV00018B/2941